THE ROMANTIC LAND OF HIND

THE ROMANTIC LAND OF HIND

By

IL MUSANNIF

(Capt. C.F. Mackenzie)

GYAN

Published by

Gyan Publishing House
5, Ansari Road
Daryaganj, New Delhi-110002
Phone: 011-47034999, 9811692060
E-mail: books@gyanbooks.com

Distribution Network
gyanbooks.com
India, USA, Canada, UK, Australia, France

ISBN : 978-81-212-6538-6 (PB)
First Published, 1882

2nd Impression 2022

Printed at: Gyan Press, Delhi.

THE ROMANTIC LAND OF HIND
Author: IL MUSANNIF (Capt. C.F. Mackenzie)

THE ROMANTIC LAND OF HIND.

BY

IL MUSANNIF
(CAPT. C. F. MACKENZIE.)

Au peu d'esprit que le bon homme avait,
L'esprit d'autrui parfois lui servait!
Il compilait, compilait, compilait!

1882.

TO THE
MEMORY OF A GREAT ORIENTALIST,
AND OF A GOOD AND KINDLY GENTLEMAN,
MY OLD PATRON AND FRIEND,

SIR HENRY MIERS ELLIOT,

ONCE SECRETARY TO THE GOVERNMENT OF INDIA,

WHOSE HUMBLE COADJUTOR I WAS IN YEARS GONE BY
IN HIS GREAT WORK
"THE MUHAMMADAN HISTORIANS OF INDIA,"
WHEN I WAS AN UNLUCKY ENSIGN OF NATIVE INFANTRY
AT PESHAWAR,
THIS SMALL BOOK OF SELECTIONS FROM THE HISTORY
OF A COUNTRY HE CREDITED ME WITH KNOWING RIGHT
WELL IS MOURNFULLY AND AFFECTIONATELY
DEDICATED BY

IL MUSANNIF, OR C. F. M.

AUTHOR'S PREFACE.

Know ye the land of the Pípal and Tulsí,*
Which Muscovites covet, but Britons will hold?
And rule it as never its own monarchs ruled it—
Those tyrannous despots of bad times of old?

The above lines, considerably altered from the "Bride of Abydos" of George Noel Gordon, Lord Byron, will, it is to be hoped, serve as a fitting introduction to this undertaking.

The various episodes which will be presented to the reader may bring before his mind's eye some of the most striking and touching events of the history of that country of Hindústán

* The *Pípal* is the species of fig known as the *Ficus religiosa*, and the *Tulsí* is the *Ocymum sanctum*, or Holy Basil.

which is still but imperfectly understood by many of the fellow-subjects of the writer.

To furnish the ground-work of this volume, ancient Oriental annalists have been had recourse to rather than European historians; and though some of the legends and tales put forward on this occasion by Il Musannif may have previously met the public eye in other versions, they may yet afford some slight satisfaction to many who take pleasure in Oriental lore, and desire to wile away a leisure hour.

IL MUSANNIF.

EDITOR'S PREFACE.

The Author of this book having died since the manuscript was placed in the publishers' hands, it has devolved upon one of his oldest surviving comrades to see it through the press; and that comrade is now called upon to confide to the public who and what manner of man the Author was.

Il Musannif—literally, the composer—or, as he was known to his friends, Captain C. F. Mackenzie, entered the military service of the East India Company thirty-eight years ago, and was posted to the 28th Regiment Native Infantry. He soon made himself remarkable for his love of the Eastern languages, more especially of Arabic and Persian; and it is scarcely too much to say that he gained a mastery over them which few have equalled. He could speak not only both, but the dialects of both, with great fluency. He could also speak and write both Turkish and Urdu with ease, besides being an accomplished French and German scholar. His acquirements in this respect were the means of introducing him to the late Sir Henry Elliot, then engaged in translating into English the manuscript histories of India. Subsequently to the death of Sir Henry Elliot, the same acquirements procured the employment of Mackenzie in the consular service in Persia.

There wanted in Captain Mackenzie but one essential quality to ensure him a brilliant success in the service of his choice. Industrious, clever, generous, versatile, and daring, he could not command his passions. His temper, when he was roused, led him to the commission of errors fatal to his advancement, and eventually caused his retirement, at an early age, from the Indian service. Subsequent to his retirement, without pension or provision, Mackenzie endeavoured to gain a precarious subsistence as a literary hack. There have been published but few great Oriental works in the Arabic and Persian languages which have not enjoyed the benefit of his great attainments. It was sad to see a man of his genius—for he really possessed genius—reduced, in the prime of life, to the verge of starvation, writing literally for a meal, and clutching at a chance sixpence. Yet such was the fate of the accomplished author of this book, translated for the most part from the original, and the compilation of which occupied those hours in which he was not writing for bare subsistence. This little work alone affords an inadequate proof of the extent of the information lost to the world when its possessor died, some few months ago, literally, from destitution.

CONTENTS.

THE ROMANTIC LAND OF HIND.

I.

AN ARAB GENERAL'S OBEDIENCE TO THE BEHESTS OF HIS KHALIF.

THE Khalífah Wálid's young general, Muhammad Kásim, had, at the early age of seventeen, attained the chief command of the Arab invaders of Hind. Though son-in-law of Hajjáj, the tyrant of Irán, his temper and policy equalled his courage and strategy; and after sweeping the whole valley of the Indus from the mountains to the sea, he is said to have penetrated as far as Kanauj.

In the year 90 of the "Departure from Mecca," he vanquished Sindh, and slew its monarch, and he planted the standard of the faith almost on the very spot where Alexander had overcome Porus!

After the capture of the hitherto impregnable fortress of Debal, Alor was taken, and its Rájá Dáhir slain; amongst the captives were the Rájá's two daughters, Súryadeo and Parmáldeo, and they were sent by the victorious general as an offering to his master at Baghdád! Fatal did the gift prove to the bestower! for when the Khalífah became enamoured of Parmáldeo's exceeding beauty, she declared herself unworthy of his attentions, because Muhammad Kásim had previously outraged both herself and her sister!

Bitter was the wrath of the Commander of the Faithful, and a hasty letter was written by his own hand to his tried and faithful servant! In this missive, which reached Muhammad Kásim at Udhápúr, it was commanded that he should be wrapt up *in the raw hide* of an ox, and so brought to Baghdád!

Calmly submissive to the decree of the despot, he allowed himself to be treated as directed, and died after three days of unspeakable torment!

The Khalífah's chamberlain, who had been the bearer of the fatal letter, then escorted the body to the capital.

The tyrant, Wálid, caused it to be carried into the apartments of the women, in order that the daughters of dead Dáhir might gloat over the corpse of the destroyer of their father!

"See," said he, "how supreme are my commands! Behold Muhammad bin Kásim!"

Then, they raised their hands, and praised and blessed the Khalífah, and said, "Kings of great justice should not proceed hastily in perilous matters, nor act precipitately upon the information of friends or enemies in the most important of all concerns. We raised this charge against Muhammad bin Kásim, out of enmity to him, because he slew our father, and because through him dominion and wealth have departed from our house; we have come as prisoners into a foreign land. The King in his anger did not weigh our words, nor distinguish between our truth and falsehood, but hurriedly issued his fatal order. The truth is, this man was to us as a father, or a brother; his hands never touched the skirts of our purity. Our object was to revenge our father, and so we made the accusation. Our wishes have been fulfilled, but there has been a serious failure in the King's justice."

Then the Chief of the Faithful, burning with anger at having been entrapped into the murder of his best and ablest officer, caused the vengeful Hindú girls to be immured alive, whilst Muhammad Kásim was magnificently entombed at Damascus.

Thus does the Arab chronicle relate the moving tale of Hindú vengeance, and of the blind fidelity of the early Musulmáns to the successors of their Prophet.

II.

THE ARABS IN HIND.

When the Khiláfat reached its highest under the great Khalífah Wálid, he sent Hárún, son of Muhammad, into Hind, to seek out those 'Allafís who had slain Sa'íd, and he enjoined him, as he valued his favour, to hunt them down like wild beasts. To this his dutiful deputy replied that, "If his life were spared to him, he would extirpate all that remained of that detestable race."

For five years he had his hands full in overcoming lands that were covered with forests, and traversed by many rivers, and when the death of the cruel and violent tyrant Hajjáj, who, although only Governor of 'Irák, was, in fact, master of the entire realm of ancient Persia, and the establishment of unity of government under Wálid, again invited the arms of the Arabs to more Eastern conquests, the decree went forth from Baghdád. The faithful girded on their swords, bestrode their steeds, and plunged onwards on their mission of destruction, under the Khalífah's lieutenant, Kutaiba, through Khwárizm, across the Oxus, and so onwards, after many an obstacle had been overcome, to Khojand, Bukhára, Shásh, and Samarkand. Even as far as Káshghar did they bear their lances, and there the men of China sent ambassadors, and prayed them to hold back their hands from the slaughter.

Kábul had fallen before a second horde, and a third body had made its way through Makrán towards the Delta of the Indus, to revenge the capture by the pirates of Debal of certain ships which the Ruler of Ceylon, or Sarandíp, had sent with gifts, pilgrims, orphan Muhammadans, and negro-slaves, as offerings to the despot of 'Irák and the Commander of the Faithful.

Who these sea-robbers were, is not precisely known, but they were probably the ancestors of the pirate Angríah, whose stronghold of Suvarndrúg was captured in the eighteenth century by that tough old British seaman, Commodore James. Their ruler was a chief named Dáhir, whom the men of Sindh obeyed.

When petitioned to take measures to hinder further ravages, the Khalífah answered that the distance and expenditure would be very great, and that he should greatly grieve to expose the lives of the faithful to such risk and peril.

The same caution had bridled fiery Musá in his onward career in Spain, and his horse with himself on it had been forcibly led back to the presence of the Khalífah at Damascus, to answer for his over-zeal.

Eastwards, the head of the Musulmáns was more yielding, and although his first general, 'Ubaidu-lla bin Nabhán, was defeated and slain at Debal, and his second envoy, Budáil, met with no better fate, the Arabs still persevered, in spite of repeated discomfitures, and the young and valiant Muhammad Kásim was their general.

As is shown in the Chách-námah, this youth, for he was beardless, with a comparatively very small force, pursued an almost broken career of conquest down the valley of the Indus. Mercy to those who bent before the new religion,—cruel death to the folk who adhered to the faith of their forefathers,—or, perchance, when savage Muhammadan bigotry was in its mildest mood, poll-tax and toleration for those who abstained from resistance.

With Muhammad Kásim were 6,000 well-chosen cavaliers from Syria, or Il Shám and 'Irák; 6,000 warriors upon camels, and a baggage-train of 3,000 camels from Khurásán.

With this force, far inferior in numbers to their innumerable opponents, and some reinforcements and supplies from that Makrán semi-desert, which was in Arab hands, Muhammad Kásim took shipping towards the port of infidel Debal.

Each of his catapults was of such mighty make, that no less than 500 men were needed to develop its powers of destruction. Such machines, borrowed from ancient Greece and Rome, had done good service to the Prophet himself at Táif, and had greatly facilitated the conquest of strong Damascus and Mecca. They had also done excellent service in Northern Africa.

The infatuated Játs and Meds helped the invaders,

and served most essentially as foot-soldiers in a land in which their cavalry were oftentimes in sorry straits, because rivers, swamps, and canals covered and intersected it.

Still, notwithstanding this much-needed and timely aid, we find the son of Islám throwing aside his Hindú followers as useless appendages when he required their services no longer, and when he had sucked the Hindú orange dry. Sumptuary laws, which prohibited the wearing of gorgeous apparel, orders for the enforced tonsure, the companionship of a dog, and other matters, soon became laws for those whose alliance had become despicable when no longer a matter of urgent need.

When the tidings came to Damascus that Muhammad Kásim had propagated the True Faith throughout the north-western provinces of Hind, and had gained incalculable booty, hosts of adventurers rushed to join in spoiling the land of the idolators. Proselytism by the strong arm, and pillage went hand in hand, so that when Muhammad Kásim went forth from Multán towards Dipálpúr and the north, he had no less than 50,000 eager adventurers beneath his banner. His conquest of such parts of Hindústán as he reached, befell in the ninety-fourth year from the "Departure," two years only after he had ridden away from Shíráz. The particulars of his sad and miserable end, Il Musannif has already told in another episode.

III.

KÁBUL UNDER RATNA-PÁL, THE HINDU.

UNDER the Khiláfat of Mu'áwiya, 'Abdu-r-rahmán, the son of Samrah, penetrated to Kábul, and for a time subdued it; but its energetic chief gathered together a number of his co-religionists and expelled the Musulmáns.

When Hajjáj, "the Sanguinary," sent 'Abdu-lla, his governor of Sístán, to exact the unpaid tribute, the wily Rájá of Kábul, Ratna-Pála, or Rutun Pál, drew back before him, blocked up the passes, crowned the heights, from which he showered down rocks and missiles of every description on the Arab host, and cut off their retreat, so that famine stared them in the face.

Loth was the fanatical son of Islám to make concessions, but necessity has no law, and he grudgingly disbursed to his Hindú foe the great sum of seven hundred thousand dirhems, to save himself and his followers from otherwise assured destruction by starvation and the sword.

To efface the disgrace inflicted on the arms of the Faithful by this signal discomfiture, Hajjáj, once more commissioned an expedition under the leadership of 'Abdu-r-rahmán bin Muhammad bin Asha's, in the seven hundredth year of our Lord.

His incursion degenerated into a mere raid or forage, and although he came back from Kábul laden with booty to Sístán, his master, the ruthless Hajjáj, was filled with ire at his not having fully carried out his commands by a thorough conquest and occupation of the country.

Exasperated by a threat of supersession, 'Abdu-r-Rahmán entered into a compact of alliance with Ratna-Pál, by which their united armies were to endeavour to bring about the fall of the tyrant Hajjáj.

Many were the vicissitudes of the struggle which ensued, and at length, when things went ill with 'Abdu-r-Rahmán, and he sought that protection from his ally which had been solemnly promised in the event of the failure of their designs, the false Hindú, after treating his guest for some time with simulated kindness and hospitality, determined to betray him into the hands of the vindictive and remorseless Hajjáj.

Well knowing what would be his fate if once surrendered to his mortal foe, 'Abdu-r-Rahmán, preferred committing suicide by casting himself from a precipice, to the torturing and lingering death which he well knew, awaited him from one who never forgave an adversary.

IV.

A WONDERFUL STONE.

THERE was a stone much believed in by the various tribes of the Turks, to which they ascribed the property of causing rain, hail, or snow, at the will of its possessor. All he had to do was, after pronouncing with all reverence the Great Name of God, to cast it into the nearest water. The first known stone of this kind, called the "Yedah," had been the gift of the archangel Gabriel to the patriarch Noah, whose son Japhet inherited it.

Turk, the son of Japhet, quarrelled with and slew his nephew,—who is reported to have been the ancestor of the Turkmáns,—for the possession of this magic stone, and then enmity and a blood-feud arose between his descendants and the Turkmáns.

When, on one occasion, according to the histories of the Mongols, Tchí-yeou raised a dense fog by its means to the bewilderment of his enemies, his adversary, Hinan-yuan, constructed a machine for indicating the south, in order to distinguish the four cardinal points. Here we have the "bezoar" stone of Eastern superstition, and the more practical mariner's compass, encompassed by a fog of Oriental legend.

The old Venetian, Marco Polo, who, after the manner of the middle ages, freely mingled the superstitions of the "Morning Land" with those of his only scarcely less benighted Italy, relates as follows:—"When in the country which borders on India, the Carannas (whoever they may have been!) wish to make an inroad and plunder, they, by their diabolical enchantment, darken the light of day so as to shroud their evil deeds."

Even the sensible Shaikh Abu-l-Fazl, that great and unfortunate Wazír of Akbar Sháh, gravely tells us that there is a lake in the mountains which divide Kashmír from Tibet, into which, if the flesh of any animal is thrown, the indignant elements will pour down showers of snow and rain on the sacrilegious offender!

When Jaipál's Hindú soldiers, in his contest with Subuktigín, quailed in that very valley of Jalálábád, now so well-known for good and evil to Her Majesty's troops, before the, to them, hitherto unwitnessed and pelting storm of snow, which paralyzed their limbs and rendered them helpless to defend themselves, they attributed the visitation to Subuktigín's employment of the "bezoar," or "yedah."

What would they have said had they witnessed the explosive wrath of the Icelandic geysers, when any foreign substance is thrust into them in these our modern days?

V.

HOW 'ABDU-R RAZÁK OF HIRÁT JOURNEYED INTO HIND.

Now the great Sultán Sháh Rukh made 'Abdu-r-Razák, the Hirátí, his ambassador to Hindústán, and he went down to the shores of the Sea of 'Umán, and to the city and port of Hurmúz, the great commercial sea-emporium at that time of all the countries of the Eastern world. Thither flocked the merchants and traders from Rúm, Persia, Tartary, China, Trans-Gangetic India, Cochin-China, Tibet, Ceylon, Hindústán, the Eastern Archipelago, and elsewhere, with every kind of merchandize under the sun.

Long detained by the soft-speaking ruler of Hurmúz, who was jealous of his embassy, for commercial and selfish reasons, 'Abdu-r-Razák, at last procured shipping, and put to sea, where, half-dead with sea-sickness, and sorely frightened by the unaccustomed perils of the deep, he and his mercantile companions sought safety, first in the port of Maskat, and then at Karíat where the intensity of the heat made them seriously ill. At length, however, he mustered sufficient courage to brave the waves once more, and eighteen days of prosperous voyage, during which the sea-breezes restored his health, brought him to the harbour of Kálikot in the land of Hind. Now the monarch of that city was called

Sámurí (the Zamorin of the Portuguese), and at his decease it was the custom to raise his sister's son to the throne. 'Abdu-r-Razák relates that this chief was as scantily clothed as his subjects, and wore merely a "langútí"; but that he occasionally bedecked himself with the most gorgeous raiment, is manifested by the relation of the Portuguese De Faria y Souza, who tells us that when Vasco de Gama and Pedro Cabral were admitted to his presence, his whole dress and person were covered with gold, pearls, and diamonds. Specially does our traveller note the custom of polyandry:—

"Among these people," says he, "is a tribe in which one woman has several husbands, of which each one engages in a separate occupation. They divide the hours of the night and day among themselves, and as long as any one of them remains in the house, during his appointed time, no other one can enter. The Sámurí is of this tribe."

The Sámurí treated the envoy with supreme contempt and neglect, and it was only after a wearisome delay that the great Hindú Rájá of Bíjánagar, sent his herald to the petty potentate of Kálikot, peremptorily requiring him to send the ambassador of the Khákán-i-Sa'íd to him without delay. "At Kálikot," remarks our traveller, "everything is procurable but beef, for should anyone be detected in the slaughter of a cow, his life would pay the penalty of the transgression. May the curse of God be on those infidels, who, to venerate this animal, have to rub the ashes of its dung upon their foreheads!" continues our pious Musulmán.

Under the safeguard of the Mahárájá of Bíjánagar, "this humble individual," as the ambassador of the Khákán deprecatingly styles himself, went on till he reached that part of Mangalore, which after having been on the first occasion abandoned by a British garrison, which ignominiously fled in 1768, before the troops of the adventurous Haidar 'Alí, and after having been retaken, but again lost to Sultán Tipú, only became a British possession in 1798, when the Maisúrí tiger fell pierced with the bayonet of a British private soldier, beneath the gateway of his own citadel of Seringapatam.

Once more on *terra firma*, to his great contentment, 'Abdu-r-Razák wended on his way through a land of wonder, and after climbing a mighty mountain, found a resting-place for a time at Bednore, where the temples, gardens, and palaces found great favour in his eyes.

Large and populous Bíjánagar surpassed all that he had hitherto beheld; governed by a potent sovereign, whose territories reached from Sarandíp (or Ceylon) to the bounds of Kulbarga, and from Bengal to Málíbár, its cultivation and fertility, and its 300 harbours, together with its elephants and 1,100,000 warriors, made its monarch the most absolute and powerful Rái in all the land of Hind.

Girt with stupendous fortifications, one within the

other, and possessing provision against a siege in the gardens and cultivated fields which existed within its limits, after the fashion of Assyrian Nineveh, its bazaars and markets teemed with wealth and abundance. In its midst rose the palace of the Rájá, and "in this charming area there were many rivulets and streams flowing through channels of cut stone, and a vast hall of many pillars, in which was the judgment-seat of the Danáík, or Administrator of the realm, and adjoining it was the Royal mint."

Numerous and pampered were the trained elephants of this great prince, and thus our narrator describes the manner of their capture:—

"A deep and large pit is dug by the path which the animal generally takes when desirous of slaking his thirst, and this is covered over with reeds and a slight coating of earth. When he falls into the trap, a man comes up and strikes him several heavy blows with a bludgeon. Suddenly another person makes his appearance, drives away the assailant, and casts away the cudgel. He then places food before the giant of the forest, and withdraws. This farce is repeated for several days, until at last the too-confiding elephant begins to regard the second man as a protector, and to take a fancy to him. Gradually he is seduced into tameness, and meekly submits to be chained and led forth by his supposed benefactor."

On one occasion these elephant-catchers met with

an elephant who was of harder mettle, and who after having been some time in bondage, had absconded from his keepers and sought refuge in the jungles. As a burnt child is said to dread the fire, this astute animal seized a stiff club with his trunk, and sounded the earth cautiously as he advanced, avoiding the pitfalls which he remembered only too vividly, until he came in safety to the stream. But at last, urged to the daring enterprize by the threats and promises of the Rájá, a mahaut ensconced himself on the branch of a tree, and thence dropped down on the back of the fugitive as he was passing towards the drinking-ford. Seizing the strong cord which they strap over the back and chest of these animals, and which had not been removed, he held it fast, and in spite of the elephant's desperate attempts to regain his freedom, he resolutely persevered in his task. When the beast threw himself on one side, in the hope of crushing his opponent, the agile keeper nimbly sprang on the side which remained uppermost, and from time to time administered several sharp blows on the head of the animal, until he gave in and was brought in triumph to the King.

Il Musannif perfectly agrees with 'Abdu-r-Razák when he says, after relating that the Rájá's 12,000 policemen were paid from the revenues derived from the taxes levied on the innumerable houses of ill-fame which prevailed in Bíjánagar, and after depicting "the splendour of these establishments, the beauty of the heart-ravishers, their blandishments and ogling," that "*it is best to be brief on the matter.*"

Royal was the hospitality afforded to the True Believer by the infidel Hindú, who gave him for abode a sumptuous mansion, "such as he recollected in his native Hirât, on the high ground near the king's gate," and where he sought repose after the fatigues of his journey during several days, until he was summoned to the presence of the Rájá.

Armed with those gifts, without which it would be both unusual and unwise to appear before a despot of the East, he beheld the Ráí seated in his forty-pillared hall, with crowds of holy Bráhmans on his right and left. He was clothed in vestments of olive-coloured satin, and round his neck was a collar of king pearls. His complexion was as olive as his garment, and he was spare, rather tall of stature, and so youthful that he had as yet neither beard nor moustache.

Received with the utmost courtesy, 'Abdu-r-Razák, who was perspiring distressfully, was allowed a superb Chinese fan to cool himself; and money, camphor, and "betel" were bestowed on him.

Nor did the hospitality of the generous Hindú end here; for daily did the Musulmán receive two sheep, four couple of fowls, five "mans" of rice, one "man" of butter, and two "varáhas" in gold.

At the time that 'Abdu-r-Razák was detained in

Kálikot, a singular and tragical occurrence took place in the city of Bíjánagar.

The King's brother, who had erected a new palace, invited the monarch and his nobles to a banquet; and as the infidels were not accustomed to eat in each other's presence, the guests were seated in a large hall, and from time to time were invited, one at a time, to partake of the viands which the host had provided.

All the drums, cymbals, trumpets, and horns in the city had been got together for this occasion, and stunning was the dissonance they produced.

When each unsuspicious victim was thus separated from his fellows, two assassins issued suddenly from their ambush, and slew him then and there; and when his remains were disposed of, another was entrapped and treated in like fashion. The noise and clangour of the drums and trumpets so effectually drowned all cries and dubious noises, that not a soul knew what had occurred, except a few fellow-conspirators of the traitorous giver of this sanguinary banquet, until almost every man of note in the state had been massacred.

While the assembly was yet reeking with the blood of the victims, the murderer went to the Rájá's palace, which he denuded of its guards by sending them off to his own mansion and entertainment, and then approaching his brother and Sovereign with a tray of "betel," in which a sharp dagger was concealed, begged him also to share the feast.

Perhaps the Rájá suspected treason, for he affected indisposition, and declined the invitation, upon which the unnatural wretch wounded him severely with his poignard and left him for dead, leaving one of his braves to cut off his head. Then rushing to the portico of the palace, he exclaimed, "I have killed the Rájá, together with his brothers, nobles, ministers, and chiefs, and now I am your king!"

But he had reckoned without his host; for when the assassin who had been detailed for the purpose had advanced to decapitate the fallen king, the latter rose as if from the dead, and after prostrating his foe by a heavy blow with a stool, made his way to the hall, where the usurper was calling on the people to acknowledge him.

The re-appearance of the rightful monarch speedily changed the aspect of affairs, and the evil-doer was instantly cast down and slain by the infuriated multitude.

When, however, the Rájá looked about him, and found that absolutely no single counsellor or relative had been left alive, his only resource was to send for his wise Danáík, who had fortunately been absent in Ceylon before the tragedy.

When tidings of this catastrophe reached the ears of the Sultán 'Alá-ud-dín, Ahmad Sháh, the ruler of

Kulbarga, he rejoiced exceedingly at the internecine quarrels of those Hindús, whose wealth and territories he coveted, as became a greedy scion of Islám; and imagining that so great a disaster, and the massacre of so many men of talent and experience, could not have failed to enfeeble the power of Deo Ráí, he ventured to send an over-bearing and insulting message to that prince.

"Pay me," said he, through his special envoy, "700,000 varáhas of gold, or I will send a world-subduing army into your country, and will extirpate idolatry down to its lowest foundations."

But the sturdy Hindú laughed at his word, and responded to his impertinent defiance by carrying war and slaughter into the country of Kulbarga itself, about the year of our Lord 1443–44, and in that of "The Departure" 847.

Crossing the Tumbadrah, suddenly, he wasted and pillaged the surrounding country as far as Ságas and Bíjápúr, and took the strong fortress of Múdkal.

Down to meet him came his Muhammadan adversary with every man he could muster; but despite the glozing of the Musulmán annalists, it is clear that the men of Kulbarga had the worst of it in three hotly contested actions, "in the first of which," says he, "multitudes were slain on both sides, *and the Hindús prevailing*, *the Musulmáns underwent heavy losses.*"

The result of the second was rather more favourable

to the Faithful, who drove back the men of Bíjánagar to shelter within the walls of Múdkal. After much bragging and boasting, however, King 'Alá-ud-dín was only too glad to accept a peace which included a mere nominal tribute, and to abstain from further aggression on the determined and persistent idolator.

To distract his mind from the disappointment which was the natural consequence of so untoward and unsatisfactory a termination of a campaign, on the successful result of which he had overweeningly counted, he devoted himself particularly to the correction of abuses and immorality in his territories. Chains were put round the necks of loafing kalandars and other idle and dissipated vagabonds, who were forced to act as scavengers in the streets, and to undergo the hardest of hard labour.

As to the wine-bibber, melted lead was poured down his throat, whatever might be his rank or station; and when the grandson of his friend, Sa'íd Muhammad, broke the laws of Islám, and not only drank to excess, but brutally maltreated a courtezan, the sinner underwent no less than two hundred bastinado-blows on the sole of his feet, and the unlucky harlot was paraded, covered with the skin of an ass, through the city, and then driven forth with contumely. Oh virtuous Sultán 'Alá-ud-dín!

Now whilst this war was in progress against the Musulmáns of Kulbarga, under the orders of that good friend of 'Abdu-r-Razák, the Wazír or Danáík, the Ráí, unhappily for the traveller, appointed as his temporary substitute a certain Hambah Murír, of whom 'Abdu-r-Razák cannot bring himself to write in terms of affection.

"He was diminutive in stature, malignant, low-born, vile, savage, and reprobate; all the most abominable qualities were united in him, and there was not an estimable trait in his composition. When the seat of administration was polluted by that wretch, he stopped my daily allowance." "Hinc illæ lachrymæ!" But worse remained behind for this sojourner in that heathen land, for the men of Hurmúz, whose insatiable lust of gain made them jealous of every interloper (as, by-the-bye, our own East India Company afterwards styled the "unchartered" whose ships came to trade in Hind in after-days), ingratiated themselves with Hambah Murír, and persuaded the Ráí that poor 'Abdu-r-Razák was no genuine ambassador of the Khákán, but had come to his Court armed with spurious documents.

However, there was a break in the clouds for a time when the good Wazír returned with spoils and Musulmán captives from his Kulbargar expedition, and much did he rate his graceless substitute for having stopped the rations of 'Abdu-r-Razák, on whom he, moreover, bestowed 7,000 fanáms on the very day of his arrival.

Two Musulmáns from Khurásán, who were residents of Bíjánagar, were deputed to accompany 'Abdu-r-

Razák on a return-embassy to his master. When the envoy had his audience of leave, the monarch told him that a rumour had spread that he was not a *boná-fide* envoy of the Sultán Mírzá Sháh Rukh, and that, should he come back with convincing proof that he was sent by so great a sovereign, he would be received with all due honour.

So 'Abdu-r-Razák packed up his belongings, and shaking the dust of Hindústán from his slippers, went towards the shore of the sea of 'Umán, and in eighteen days arrived at the harbour of Mangalúr, in January, A.D. 1444, whence, after seeking a "fál," or omen, from the holy Kurán, in which he found the appropriate verse, "Be not afraid, for you have been rescued from the tribes of wicked men," he embarked once more.

His account of this sea-trip is so thoroughly that of an Oriental landsman, that Il Musannif cannot refrain from quoting it:—

"Sometimes," he writes, "we were engaged in conversation on the extraordinary events and wonderful appearances which had come under our observation, and our hearts enjoyed peace and contentment. Sometimes from the effect of contrary winds, which resembled drunkards, the cup of vicissitude found its way into the vessel, and its planks which were so joined as to resemble a continuous line, were on the point of becoming separate, like isolated letters of the alphabet."

When a raging tempest which overtook the voyagers

had lulled, and the sea had calmed down to their heart's desire, they sighted, at the end of Zí-hijja, the mountain-ridges of Kalahát; and after repairing damages at Maskat, they reached the port of Khúrfakán, "where the night was so hot that, when dawn broke, you might have said that the sky had set the earth on fire, and where the strong-winged bird of the air, and the fish in the depths of the sea, were equally scorched by the heat!"

From thence, with no interruption, they securely reached the haven of Hurmúz, after having been exposed to the perils of the ocean five-and-seventy days.

It would not take a British steamer quite so long to complete the same voyage, for navigation and science are not now-a-days so crude and imperfect as they were when 'Abdu-r-Razák first journeyed into Hind!

VI.

THE ECCENTRIC SÚMRÁS.

Now, if the annalist, Mír Táhir Muhammad Nasyání, of Thatta, who was himself a man of Sindh, is worthy of credence, the Súmrás were a most peculiar people. One of them, Dúda Súmrá, killed all his brothers who refused to submit to become his bondsmen; and it was fashionable to have the nails of the hands and feet extracted by the barber *from the roots*.

When asked why they underwent such uncalled-for and unnecessary torture in gaiety of heart, they answered that they were not as other men, and could do what the rest of their species were incapable of doing.

Clothes once worn were cast aside and never resumed; and when a man's wife had become a mother she never again shared his couch.

A Súmrá woman, when about to be brought to bed, and who felt distracted at the prospect of the severance between her and her much-loved lord and master, which would inevitably ensue the moment their offspring saw the light, meditated how to convince him that child-birth did not render a female impure. In pursuance of the plan she had conceived, she gave all the clothes which her husband took off to the washerman with strict injunctions to cleanse them with great care.

One day, when he had taken a bath, he called for linen to dry his limbs, and some which had been washed and laid aside was given to him. "What new cloths are these," said he, "for they are unusually soft?" and when his wife explained, he declared his intention of wearing washed clothes for the future.

"Such then," said his spouse, "is the condition of women, and why should men abjure their society when they have undergone purification?"

The husband admitted the error of his former ways, and the whole tribe followed his example.

But this little anecdote proves that the eccentric Súmrás possessed at least the virtue of cleanliness.

Well would it be were other Eastern nations, Turks, Arabs, Persians, and Afghâns, to wit, to do likewise, and not to wear foul garments, which remain with them until the tattered remnants literally *walk* off their backs.

Little benefit do they derive from their frequent baths and ablutions, when they invariably re-cover their freshly-cleansed bodies with the same verminous raiment.

VII.

A FIERY ORDEAL.

Now when 'Umar, the Súmrá, governed in Sindh, he imitated not the virtues and chastity of his namesake, that sturdy and bigoted early Apostle of Islám who overcame Syria and burned the great Alexandrine Library, who contented himself during his most trying campaigns with the dates and rude habiliments of his forefathers of the desert, and whose name, although in the odour of sanctity amongst Sunní sectaries, is an abomination and a stench in the nostrils of the Shíahs of Persia.

No married woman or maiden whom he coveted escaped from his licentious clutches.

Now there was a woman whose name was Márúí, inasmuch as she was one of the Márúís, who dwelt in the wastes about 'Umar-Kot, and who were known as the "Wanderers of the Desert." Her betrothed, the youth Phag, had been discarded, and her parents had bestowed her in marriage on a relative.

In revenge, the forsaken one sought the licentious 'Umar, and, after lauding the beauty of Márúí, urged him to seize her for himself. Ever ready to listen to advice which accorded so well with his own debauched inclinations, the chieftain of the Súmrás mounted a swift camel, and roughly carried off his unwilling prize to his citadel.

Vainly did he attempt to win the consent of the chaste wife, who spurned his presents and derided his cruel anger, until at last her unswerving fidelity to her conjugal duty during an entire year of captivity, softened the heart of the abductor.

Sending at the end of that period for the injured husband, he restored him his wife together with great gifts; but the husband did not credit his fair wife's purity, and vilified and harshly abused her.

'Umar's indignation when this came to his ears exceeded all bounds, and he despatched a force to punish the Márúí tribe, which, however, decamped on hearing of his approach and escaped into the trackless wilds.

Brave Márúí, however, dared to present herself

before the despot and to say, "But for your unjust behaviour in the first instance towards me, when you detained me as your prisoner for twelve long months, my husband would have had no cause for suspicion and jealous anger."

Moved by her words 'Umar consented that the Hindú oath and ordeal of fire should be resorted to in order to convince the unbelieving husband of the unblemished chastity of his ill-treated spouse.

A fire was kindled and a bar of iron made red-hot therein.

The hand of Márúí remained unscorched and uninjured when she lifted the glowing metal from the flames! then were the Hindús the first to acknowledge her to be a stainless wife; and 'Umar, farther to bring conviction to the man he had so injured, bravely passed, dressed as he was, through the raging fire.

"Glory to God!" says the author of the Táríkh-i-Táhiri, "not a hair of his head or a thread of his garment were singed, and he issued scathless from the flames which consume alike friend and foe." 'Umar and the relatives of the virtuous wife, whom idle-talkers had calumniated and reviled, were now raised in public opinion; the doubts which had tormented the husband vanished, and his unkind treatment ceased.

It is to be hoped, although of 'Umar's future conduct we have no record, that, in view of this disagreeable ordeal, he abstained in after days from coveting his neighbours' wives, and became a pattern of morality to his subjects.

VIII.

A LOSING TWO-DICE GAME, OR A HINDÚ STORY OF A COCK AND BULL.

Now when Yudhishthira and his mighty Pándava brethren had brought all the reigning monarchs with their treasure from the conquered lands of Khatai, Rúm, and all the regions of the world, to their great city, Indraprashtha, the envy of the race of the adverse Kauravas waxed exceedingly, and Duryodhana, after much crafty counsel, enticed the open-hearted and unsuspicious sons of Pándu to gamble with him at the game of "páshá," which is played with two dice, for unheard-of stakes. The black-leg, Duryodhana, so deceived his guests that their losings were enormous.

But on their ruin, he proposed as last stake of all, that if they won they should receive back all they had hitherto lost, but that in the event of further ill-fortune, they should forsake their homes and habitations and dwell in the jungle, with no companionship but that of the beasts and feathered tribes for the long space of twelve years.

To these hard conditions was added another stipulation, that they should seek their livelihood in disguise for yet one year more, and that if they should be recognised by anyone, they should endure the hardships of a forest-life for another twelve years.

Having lost their last wager to the unrighteous Kaurava, like true men the Pándavas kept to their unlucky bargain, and when their twelve years of penance came to an end, they made their way to the district of Wáín, which is near Sitárá in the "Southern Land."

From thence they sent Srí Krishna, (that since deified Apollo of the Hindús, and the beloved of the Gopís or "Milk-maids,") as their ambassador, to demand the restitution of their lands from the false and crafty Duryodhana; who heeded not their just appeal.

Then, in the earlier times of the "Black Age," the rival armies met at the lake of Kuru-Kshetra, near Tháneswar, and between the deserted British cantonment of Karnál and the camp of Lúdhíána.

Eighteen days did the battle endure, and fearful was the slaughter, but in the end the Machiavellian Duryodhana and his allies perished almost to a man, although their adversaries fared but little better, seeing that, according to that veracious history the "Mahábhárata," only twelve men on either side remained alive, of whom Srí Krishna was one.

This celebrated person, foster-son of Nanda, the tender of cattle, was born in Mathurá, and is stigmatized by many of the Hindús as the greatest and most unscrupulous rogue and cheat in the universe, contrived to kill the Rájá Kans, chief of the Yádavas, and to seat himself on his throne.

He, afterwards, pretended to be of divine origin, and myriads of credulous Hindús became his proselytes, and his pranks and libidinous deeds, extending over a space of upwards of thirty years, are they not written in hyperbolic and exaggerated diction in that "Sea of Love," the "Prem-Ságar," in which stupid superstition and licentious filth are equally mingled?

The Rájá Jarásandha, who ruled over Bihár, marched against Krishna's capital, Mathurá; and another foe to the lewd impostor, who was a "Mlechha" (or one of those who were *not* born in the exclusive Hindú faith, and was consequently regarded as an "outside barbarian"), came up from the countries of the west.

Seventy-eight years, says the *truthful* annalist, did Srí Krishna hold out in his strong coast-fortress of Dwáriká; but at last, and when he was 125 years old, quite a youth in fact in those remote Hindú days, he came to an *untimely* and premature end by assassination at the instigation of the vindictive mother of the late Duryodhana.

The "Prem Ságar," in its first lines, only speaks of

his "disappearance," unwilling to admit that the cherished divinity of the lustful idolaters should have partaken of the common lot of mortal men.

So full of legend and myth are the ante-Muhammadan Hindú writings, that the student will scarcely discover a grain of truth in the ocean of popular romance which the Hindús dignify by the grand name of *History*; we therefore, as a rule, adhere to those events and episodes which we find in Musulmán chronicles, from the first invasion of Hind by the Arabs of Wálid down to the death of Aurangzeb.

IX.

THE LOVES OF SASSÍ AND PANNÚN.

Now the holy Bráhman, Náníya, and his wife, Mundhar, who dwelt in Bhámbarwárá, beneath the rule of Rájá Dalu, were desirous of offspring, and when a daughter was born to them, who was "the envy of the full moon," a revelation came to her parents that she was destined to become the bride of a Musulmán. Dreading so great a disgrace, her father shut her up in a box, "like a pearl in its shell," and cast her into the river.

Now fortune willed that the current of the stream should bear the poor little waif to the city of Bhambúr, in which dwelt the rich washerman, Lála Náníya, who, although he boasted of 500 assistants in his trade, was a childless man.

When his apprentices brought him the box from the bank of the river, where they had discovered it whilst pursuing their avocation after the fashion of Hind, he opened it, and, struck with pity for the foundling, adopted it as his own, and gave it the name of Sassí, or "the Moon."

As she grew up, all people were spell-struck by her charms, of which all coveted the possession; "wherever she seated herself men crowded round her like the cluster of the Pleiades."

When the caravans from Kích and Makrán arrived at Bhambúr with their merchandize, young Pannún, the son of the Chief of Kích, beheld fair Sassí and surrendered his heart to her, whilst she, on her side, became enamoured of the handsome young stranger.

To be near to his beloved and to have a chance of meeting her, he assumed the garb and disguise of a washerman, and became an apprentice of her adopted father.

Now the wicked wife of a goldsmith, who had also fallen in love with good-looking Pannún, with an unholy and sensual affection, sought to bring about a separation between the lovers by exciting Pannún's jealousy; but her malignant efforts were unsuccessful, "and the devoted girl passed through the ordeal, like gold through the raging fire," and was at last married to Pannún.

Pannún's father was a bigoted Musulmán, and in order to free his son from the enthralment of his Hindú bride, he, with the aid of his other sons, bore away the sleeping husband from the arms of his unsuspecting spouse.

When the unhappy Sassí awoke and found that she had been robbed of her living treasure, she wailed and tore her garments, and set off in quest of the lost one.

"With the feet of affection" she traversed the rugged hills, and after accomplishing a distance of about forty "kos," she fell exhausted from thirst, and was convulsed, striking her feet on the ground as if in the agony of death. By the power of God, she found a pool of water, and she drank and revived. Continuing on her way some six or seven "kos" further, she again was harassed by thirst, and was saved by her gentle appeals for forbearance from the hands of a rough shepherd, who, although he had at first made up his mind to maltreat her, subsequently relented for a while, and went to fetch milk to refresh the fainting damsel.

Fearing he would renew his loathsome advances on his return, the despairing Sassí, who had no longer any hope of again beholding her beloved Pannún, vented the anguish of her heart before the Almighty (who is the Comforter of the helpless).

Then, by a miraculous interposition, the hill was rent asunder, and the distressed Sassí found a refuge in its bosom. The wicked shepherd, when he beheld this marvel, repented him of his evil intentions, and placed a heap of stones to mark the spot where the abyss had just closed on Sassí.

Now when Pannún, who had been brought in chains before his father, showed such symptoms of grief and restlessness, that his reason was looked on as endangered, his father yielded, and sent him, in company with his brothers, to seek the lost Sassí.

Arriving at the spot of her entombment, and learning the strange prodigy from the shepherd, Pannún dismounted from his camel, and went toward the heap of stones.

Casting himself on the ground, he cried aloud to the Almighty, beseeching that he might be joined to his love.

As no petitioner before God is ever left without hope, the hill at once opened and admitted Pannún, and he and his "mistress were encased like twin-almonds in one shell."

This most veracious story of unhappy affection still finds believers at Husaini and elsewhere in the parched up land of Sindh.

X.

A HINDUSTANI FEMALE FIEND.

In the days of Sultán Ibráhím, when there was abundance in the land of Hind, a tradesman of the town of Sámána chanced to be summoned from his house on pressing business, and when he departed he gave charge of his house to a trusty friend and neighbour who used frequently to visit the dwelling in order to advise and assist the wife of the absentee in her household concerns.

Becoming aware that a young and good-looking youth was frequently a visitor there, and reflecting that he could be no relation of the owner of the house, the neighbour's mind became filled with suspicion that something wrong was going on, and in order to satisfy his doubts, he secretly pierced a hole through the partition-wall which divided his friend's dwelling from his own, and kept a close watch.

One night he saw a youth dressed in white and much scented with perfumes, enter and seat himself on a carpet near the merchant's wife, with whom he revelled on sweetmeats, wine, and betel-nut, and at length, broke the law of Islám in most criminal fashion.

Now this female had a child, which slept in another room, and as it worried her with its wailing, she strangled the unhappy brat with her own hands, and then returned serenely to the embraces of her lover.

When interrogated by the adulterer why the child had not made itself heard for such a length of time, she coolly informed him that she had taken steps to prevent it from crying altogether.

This disturbed the young man greatly, and he said to this female fiend, "O creature, without fear of God, for the sake of a moment's pleasure you have destroyed the fruit of your own womb; how, then, can I rely on you?"

So saying, he began to dress himself with the intention of leaving the place, but she seized his skirt, saying, "For you I have done this, and now you would cease to love me. For God's sake aid me to conceal my shame, by digging a hole in the room wherein to bury the murdered child."

Reluctantly did he consent, and when he had dug a grave with a mattock which she provided, she brought the child and handed it to him, and as he bent down unsuspectingly for the purpose of placing it in the hole, she raised the mattock and dealt him such a stroke from behind that his skull was split in two, and he fell dead into the grave.

Hastily covering up both corpses and carefully smashing down the earth, she began to wail and lament, exclaiming, "A wolf has devoured my child."

Now, such a statement might have passed current,

especially in the wilder parts of Hind, where it is of no unfrequent occurrence to hear of children being snatched away by prowling wolves, even in these days of Anglo-Indian rule; but, unfortunately for the scheme of this she-devil, the neighbour had been a shocked witness of the whole horrible affair from his observatory.

Still, he kept his counsel until the return of his friend, the husband, from his journey, and having invited him privately to his own house, he revealed the history of the slaughter of both the child and the youth. "Then," he continued, "in order to prove the truth of what I relate, do you pretend that you had in former days buried some gold within your apartment, and procure a mattock to dig it up with."

When the unfaithful woman saw that he immediately began to dig in the spot which the neighbour had pointed out to him, and knew that her dreadful secret was on the eve of being laid bare, she fastened the door of the room in which her husband was delving, and set fire to the thatch of the roof; then, with combined cunning and hypocrisy, exclaiming "Come to my assistance, for the house is in flames, and my husband in peril of his life," she hied to the neighbours, who came all too late, for the unhappy victim of conjugal perfidy and cruelty had already been burnt to death.

The neighbour who had witnessed this fresh atrocity went with others to the Kotwâl, or chief police magistrate, and told all he knew, so that search was made, and the bodies of the youth and child were brought to the light of day.

Upon this the wrathful citizens proceeded to wreak their vengeance upon "this bloody-minded woman," whom they buried in the "bázár" up to her waist, and then goaded with arrows till she died.

And this tragedy is still known in Sámána as "The threefold murder, by one woman, in one house."

XI.

SUPPRESSION OF A TURKI REVOLT IN DEHLI.

A short and sweet description of the suppression of a Turkish revolt in Dehlí, by that same worthy scribe, Hasan Nizámí, is now given by Il Musannif, in order to show how great a waste of pen-reeds and exceedingly "oily" ink arose from the adulations and embellishments of comparatively petty deeds, from the hands of subservient and time-serving annalists.

Sir-jándár, the seditious Turk, opened his hands to shed the blood of the Faithful, and, backed by bloodthirsty comrades of his own race, rebelled openly, and the Sultán, after having "refrained from repressing this violence" (probably from very prudential reasons), at last made up his mind to send his most valiant warriors against them.

"This force of fiery courage, and swift as is the wind, stood like a bulwark of steel near the gardens which lined the banks of the Jamna, and after a terrible contest, in which many a chieftain perished, the head of the insurrection, Sir-jándár Turkí, threw himself into the waters of the Jún (as the Muhammadans styled the Jamna), took flight like a fox who is in dread of a lion, and departed tremulously down the course of the river and across the hills, as would have done a crocodile or a leopard, and concealed himself in the deep jungles, like a sword in a scabbard, or a pen in a writing-case (such as the scribes of India wear in their girdles, dagger-fashion)."

It goes without telling, in Gallic phrase, that his abettors were all either put to the sword or scattered abroad.

XII.

THE KARMATIAN HERETICS.

THE religion of Islám had no sooner become a power than divisions, feuds, and schisms broke out among its professors, as appears to have ever been the case with all new creeds. The fervid Eastern temperament, exalted by victory and by the intolerant doctrines of Muhammad, impelled his followers to unparalleled excesses.

The overthrown but uneradicated superstitions of former religions, and the mystic theology and philosophy of the nations with which the Musulmáns came in contact, helped to produce and develop heresies, but their active political importance was mainly due to a thirst for distinction and worldly power.

Thus the principal divisions turn upon the rightful succession to the Prophet in the office of "Commander of the Faithful."

The Karmatian sect was a branch of the Ismáílian heresy, and so slight were the doctrinal differences of the two that the uninitiated confounded them together.

Whilst orthodox Muhammadans maintain that certain Imáms were the rightful successors of Muhammad, the Ismáílians only acknowledge 'Alí, Hasan, and Husain, and aver that the line came to an end in the person of Ismáíl, bin Ja'far Sádik, the seventh and last of the "Imáms." From him they derive their name of *Ismáílian*, and from him, likewise, they are styled "Seveners." By them the Kurán was metaphorically interpreted, its doctrines were explained away or superseded, and a mere negative religion remained in which morality gave way to license.

The Persian Abdu-llah, son of Maimún, embraced their doctrines and devoted his every energy to the subversion, not only of Arab supremacy, but of all religion. By secret influence and untiring missionary enterprise, he sought to attain his ends. All religions were vanities in his eyes, and he preached that, whilst the good received no reward, the wicked remained unpunished both in this world and the next.

Amongst his disciples was one Ahmad, subsequently called "Karmat," who, about the year of the Christian era, 891, founded the sect since known by his name. "Karmat" was a peculiar writing in use amongst the Arabs, the obscurity of which well fitted it for secret correspondence. Teaching that every desire might be lawfully indulged, he differed from his predecessors by the violent mode in which he spread his tenets abroad, and there was soon an open and unsparing struggle between him and the rulers of the period.

More than two centuries after "the Departure," he made a terrible inroad into Syria, and twenty-one years later he sacked Basrá and Kúfa. In the year 909–10 A.D., the renowned Ismáilian general, Abú Táhir, took Mecca with terrible slaughter, and carried away and kept for twenty years the holy "Hijru-l-Aswad," or "Black Stone." The twentieth of the line of the Khalífahs of Baghdád, Ar-Rází, was fain to pay them annual black-mail, to secure the safety of the pilgrims on their road to Mecca and Madínah, and in 297 A.H. one of their number founded the Fatimide dynasty in Egypt, where its power soon became an object of fear and jealousy to those who sat on the throne of Baghdád, so that both parties, stirred by religious hatred, carried on a savage and unrelenting war.

Perhaps the most noteworthy off-shoot of the sect of the Ismáilians was that which forced itself on the Crusaders, and first introduced the word "assassin" into the languages of Europe. Whether this word was derived from "Hashíshin," or "Hemp-Eater," from the stimulant of "bhang" or "hashish" with which fanatics infuriate themselves for desperate deeds, or whether they derived the appellation from the name of their founder, Hasan Sabah, of the old city of Rhe in 'Irák, are moot points and are likely to remain so.

The forcible removal of all foes and rivals by the daggers of the "Hashíshins" was the distinctive rule of this abominable sect, and in 483 A.H. Hasan Sabah established himself in the mountain stronghold of Alámút, or the "Eagle's Nest," in the district of Rúdbár, and near the confines of Gílán, where I, Il Musannif, sat one day in the year of grace 1858, and meditated on the strange deeds of which that ruined and craggy spot had been the scene in the far away past.

For two centuries did these bandits maintain their hold on Alámút, until it fell before the wild hordes of Hulákú Khán, who spared neither man, woman, nor infant at the breast.

The Karmatians would seem to have made their way eastward at an early period, and were settled in Multán when Mahmúd of Ghazní assailed that city.

The Afghán monarch's own prime minister Hasirak was brought to the stake on a charge of favouring this heterodox creed, and Mahmúd hounded down and impaled every Karmatian he fell in with; but could not root out the stubborn heresy, and at a far later period, 1237 A.D., we find a strong band of Karmatians making a desperate onslaught on the faithful who were assembled at prayer in the Great Mosque of Dehlí; on this occasion, though, they fared but ill, for they were finally overpowered, and, as a very forcible Mahammad scribe relates, "every heretic and Karmatian was sent to hell."

XIII.

HOW THE SULTÁN MAHMÚD DESTROYED SOMNÁTH.

When the Sultán heard of the great reverence paid to the idol-god of Somnáth, and how 3000 Bráhmans worshipped daily at its shrine, whilst 300 barbers shaved the heads and beards of thousands of pilgrims, and 150 "Náchnís" sang and danced at the gates of the temple, he resolved to carry a holy war into that region.

So, after praying to the Almighty for aid, he began his march from Ghazní on the tenth day of Sha'bán, in the year of "the Departure" 414, with an array of 3,000 cavaliers, besides volunteers, and took the road to Multán.

From that city, which he reached during the fast of Ramazán, his path lay through a barren and uncultivated waste to the rich land of Hind.

Traversing this wilderness with great difficulty and hardship—for he was, of necessity, the bearer of his own provisions—he stormed a strong fortress, and heeding not the submission of the idolators, steeped his unsparing sword in their blood, and destroyed their images of stone and metal, as became a ruthless apostle of "the Religion of the Sword."

In the beginning of Zí-l-Káda, his swarm of savage fanatics fell on the devoted town of Anhalwárá, but its chief, Rái Bhím, took flight at the appoach of the Musulmáns, who scattered themselves abroad throughout the country, slaying without pity every Hindú they encountered, and destroying every graven image they found. One great army of some 20,000 were dispersed as is chaff by the hurricane, and Dabalwárá, in spite of a stubborn resistance, shared the fate which had befallen all previous opponents of the monarch of Ghazní.

In two days more he beheld the strong fortress-temple of Somnáth, with its walls washed by the waves of the ocean.

The Hindús of Somnáth derided their enemies from the summit of their many fortifications, and scoffingly told them that the great god of the Hindús would surely annihilate the fanatical aggressors of his shrine.

Ill did they weigh their words when they calculated on a certain victory over the stern Muhammadans, who, valiantly planting their ladders, took the outer walls by assault, and drove the flying Hindú defenders into the recesses of their sanctuary.

Raising the war-cry of Islám, the soldiers of Mahmúd shed blood in oceans, and after strewing the earth with the corpses of the slain, awaited the dawn of the morrow before renewing their attack on the main stronghold.

Fierce and desperate were the Hindú braves who were pent therein; and casting themselves in supplication before their much-revered idol, they prayed all night to Somnáth for victory.

Then, after the fashion of their race, and of which there are unhappily too many examples in their struggles with the intolerant sons of Islám, in the blood-stained pages of Mahammadan-Indian histories, they devoted themselves to an almost certain death by rushing, sword in hand, on the invaders, neither giving nor accepting quarter. None did they receive, and the carnage ceased not until but very few remained, and these were reserved for conversion to the creed of the victors and to a bitter and grinding serfdom.

'Ibn Asír, or the "Son of the Captive," tells us that the number of the slain amounted to the grim total of 50,000—a fitting holocust offered up by the followers of the Man of Mecca as a grateful sacrifice to the Almighty.

Now the idol of Somnáth, which had proved so frail a protector to its too trustful worshippers, was of stone, and some five yards in stature, and when the "Ghází" Mahmúd beheld it, his bosom was so filled with pious wrath and indignation, that he dashed the imposture to pieces with that good battle-axe which few others could wield.

This did he in spite of the enormous offers of the Hindú priests, who proffered untold wealth if he would relent and abstain from mutilating their much-revered deity; and well was his fanaticism rewarded, for when the image had been demolished it was found to contain so many precious stones and jewels that their value exceeded a hundred times the ransom which the astute and wily Bráhmans, who well knew of this secret deposit, had offered him.

Then he commanded that the fragments of the image should be carried to his own great city of Ghazní, and placed before the threshold of its chief mosque, the "Jam'i Masjid," that all might behold the evidence of his great and successful zeal for that creed of Blood which the Camel-Driver of Mecca had imposed upon so large a portion of the Eastern world.

XIV.

PETTICOAT GOVERNMENT; OR, "HELL HATH NO FURY LIKE A WOMAN SCORNED."

When the country of Khwárizm fell under the sway of Mahmúd, the Sultán, he enjoined his Wazírs and "the Pillars of his Court" to find some able Musulmán to rule it.

After deep and repeated councils, it was conferred on Altúntásh (which means, in the Turkish tongue, "the Stone of Gold") who was the very "noble of nobles" of the Court of the Founders of the Ghaznawí dynasty.

In spite of many despicable intrigues,—the aim and object of which was to debar Altúntásh from this satrapy,—the Sultán issued his final decree that he should proceed to assume the reins of the Government of Khwárizm.

Ere he departed, he entreated, by letter, his nearest and most familiar friend, the holy Imám, Násiru-d-dín Girámí, to renew their amicable relationship by paying him a lengthened visit in the seat of his new Government. Accordingly, the Imám joined him there, and was treated as a bosom-friend.

Now the influence of Chief "Golden Stone" had been hitherto so vast at a Court where all the world humbly besought his protection, that the power and pecuniary advantages of his position exceeded by many times the emoluments and advantages of the Government of Khwárizm.

When questioned, then, by his friend concerning his inexplicable acceptance of so inferior a post, he remarked, "O Imám, I have not revealed this mystery even to my own sons or dearest friends, but from you I have nothing to conceal. I have resigned on account of that base female-favourite of the King, Jamílah Kandahárí. For years I had the management of all affairs of government, and during that time she thwarted me in everything. For this reason there was darkness before my eyes, and I could find no remedy against the evil. Now I have sought retirement, and have secured release from all such troubles. If God please, I shall escape her machinations in this distant province."

So the great Khán fled before a "Záífah" (or "Weak one"), as the Persians genteelly call a lady, and was greatly rejoiced when he found safety in a remote city from the artifices of "*the Beautiful One from Kandahár.*"

"Now, from what I have said," sagely remarks the author of the above anecdote, "the disadvantage of being in opposition to the royal ladies is only too evident;

but if they are in our favour, great benefits accrue to us, and no one's patronage is more efficacious than theirs, and no other person has such influence over the mind of the king as they."

And that this same influence has not yet died out amongst Musulmáns, the present condition of Istámbul and of Turkey will fully illustrate.

XV.

THE LOVE OF SULTÁN MAHMÚD FOR THE SISTER OF AYÁZ.

Not always was the soul of the ruler of Ghazní moved by the aspirations of ambition and the lust of conquest alone; for one evening, as he reposed on his couch after ridding himself of his servile courtiers and of the cares of State, he thus addressed his confidential attendant, Abú Nasr Mishkání, "Oh, friend!" said the monarch, "wise men have told us that from three sorts of persons we should have no concealment, but reveal our innermost secrets to them; the first is an able physician, the second a kindly preceptor, and the third a trustworthy and wise servant. Now I require your truthful opinion on a subject with which my mind has been so long and sorely perplexed that I can rest no longer without sound counsel. I have long had a hankering after the sister of Ayáz; but will my taking her to wife not entail on me the contempt not only of other monarchs, but of my own domestics and servants? Can you lay before me any instance in which a sovereign wedded the daughter of his slave?"

Then, with the usual oriental accompaniment of a profound reverence, the politic courtier Abú Nasr thus replied, and, as he spoke, he shampooed the King:

"Many kings of the Sámánian dynasty married the daughters of their slaves, and in the time of Kubád, when he was in Turkistán, he espoused a village girl, who became the mother of Naushírwán 'the Just.'

"In the annals of Irán it is written that Bahrám Gúr married the daughter of a plebeian washerman, and that their union took place in this wise:

"One day, whilst engaged in the chase, Bahrám was separated from his train by the eager pursuit of a stag, and coming athirst to a village he espied a washerman washing clothes in a pool, in company with his wife and daughter.

"When they recognised the monarch they humbly and respectfully brought the bowl of water he had asked for, and, said the elder female to her daughter, 'I am no virgin, but you, who are an unblemished pearl, may well serve the King with drink.' So charmed was Bahrám Gúr with the beauty and grace of his cup-bearer, that he even stayed to dine on the dry bread which was all that the poor cleanser of clothes could offer him, whilst the fair damsel stood beside him and fanned away those plagues of flies which abound in Eastern lands; but finding his repast not sufficiently succulent, he brought food, wine, meat, and everything that came to hand, from the village, and made strong love to the low-born lassie. When she kissed his hands, quoth Bahrám Gúr, gallantly and tenderly, 'Oh, maiden! lips, and not hands, should be kissed.' 'No,' answered the modest girl, 'the time has not come for that,' and as she spoke the King's retinue appeared in sight."

The long and short of this apologue is, that he married her on the spot, placed her beneath a royal canopy on an elephant, and carried her and her whole family with kingly state to his palace.

This story so thoroughly convinced Sultán Mahmúd that his dignity would in no wise suffer from espousing the sister of Ayáz, that he married the lady two days after, and whether his high position and her own elevation compensated his wife for the personal ugliness of Mahmúd, ancient writers do not report.

XVI.

THE GOOD DÁBSHILIM AND HIS NAMESAKE.

WHEN all the country of Somnáth had submitted to Mahmúd, the Warrior Sultán of Ghazní, with prudent policy he selected a certain Dábshilim from amongst the natives of the land, to act as his deputy and remit annual tribute to the seat of his Empire.

Now this Dábshilim, who was a very wise, virtuous, and intelligent man, and who accepted the trust confided to him, had an ill-conditioned relative with whom he was on the worst of terms, whose antagonism he dreaded after the Sultán's departure to Ghazní.

But Mahmúd settled matters by seizing Dábshilim the Second and handing him over to Dábshilim "the Good."

It was an amiable custom of those times in Hind to stow a conquered and captive enemy in a dismal and narrow dungeon immediately under the throne of the king, and to convey daily a dish of food to him through a hole in the door which was never opened.

As the heart of the gentle Dábshilim revolted at having recourse to so tyrannical a measure, which would assuredly have brought the prisoner to a lingering death, he besought the Sultán Mahmúd to carry the man back with him to Ghazní pending the settlement of the affairs of the country on a solid basis; and this was done.

The pious Dábshilim now ruled in Somnáth, and duly forwarded the stipulated tribute, with many rich presents for the monarch and his "Wazírs."

Then Dábshilim the Second, after a certain stay in Afghánistán, was sent back to India; and as it was customary for the rulers of that period on the approach of a captured foe, to proceed a day's march from their chief city to meet and drive him before their horses to his place of durance, Dábshilim the Good went forth for this purpose.

As, however, the report of his namesake's arrival proved to be premature, Dábshilim the Pious disported himself with hunting in order to wile away the time, but the hot winds were exceedingly strong, and he was compelled to seek shelter with his followers beneath a tree, by which he fell asleep.

Now one of those greedy birds of carrion, known as "chíls" or kites, who are to this day to be seen in myriads in every part of Hindústán, espying the red handkerchief with which Dábshilim had covered his face, and mistaking it for raw meat, swooped down upon it in hawk-fashion, and in clutching it, tore out the eyes of the sleeper, who thus became ineligible for Government, and was replaced in authority by his now victorious enemy, who did not forget to secure him in the subterranean cell. *Sic transit gloria mundi.*

XVII.

TWO CAPTURES OF KOT KÁNGRÁ.

Some miles beyond the Biyáh or Biyás River, on the banks of which are the Fire-Temples of Jwálá-Mukhí (or "the Mouth of Flame"), stands the once impregnable fortress of Nagar-Kot, or Kot Kángrá, by both of which names it is well-known to Hindú pilgrims to this day.

Rising many hundred feet above two mountain-torrents, the Bán Gangá and the Pátál Gangá, which wash the base of its stupendous rock, the citadel towers over the tranquil pool known as the "Sangam" (or "Meeting of the Waters"), where Il Musannif, who was some thirty years ago an unimportant member of the British garrison of that renowned stronghold, has often fished placidly for the great "Mahá-Sar," regardless of slovenly, unhandsome, and half-roasted Hindú corpses which occasionally floated by as he angled.

From the citadel, now bearing the Muhammadan epithet of the "Shísh-Mahall," the buildings, more or less ruined, slope down in step-like fashion to the petty town of Kángrá.

Save and excepting myriads of large "langúr" apes, and of their impudent and smaller short-tailed congeners, the large area of the fort is a jungle and a wilderness, and has no human inhabitants but the small garrison necessary to defend so important a post.

Commanded as it is by the surrounding heights, it easily fell before the eighteen-pounders which the force of poor Sir Hugh Wheeler dragged against it over the passes which intervened between it and the plain of the Jálandhar Dúáb, after the first Punjáb campaign, and has lost its character of impregnability.

A mile northward lies holy Bháwan, or the Temple of Saktí. Kángrá, or, as it was then called, Bhímnagar, was captured by Mahmúd of Ghazní, owing to the pusillanimity of its defenders, "who fell on their faces like sparrows before a hawk, or rain before lightning," as Al Atbi boastingly relates.

Being the repository of the belongings of all the neighbouring Rájás, the booty captured in Kángrá was naturally immense. Stamped coin to the amount of 70,000 royal dirhems, and gold and silver ingots of 700,400 "mans," with great spoil of rich clothing, and a silver shrine thirty yards in length and fifteen in breadth, besides other valuables, were borne away by the triumphant conqueror to Ghazní.

Truly, the zeal of those old Mahammadans was as much stimulated by the love of gain as by their desire of proselytism to the tenets of their murderous creed.

XVIII.

IL MUSANNIF'S OWN TRANSLATIONS FROM THE DÁÚDI ANNALS.

Olim meminisce juvabit; so, forgetting sad and sorry treatment at the hands of people who were possessed of less heart, generosity, and talent than their progenitor, who was as good-looking as he was talented, Il Musannif picks up some of those translations which he had made with his own hands under the burning sky of unwholesome Peshávar, in 1850–51, for the sake of one who would have been his benefactor had he lived.

Historians who have written concerning the reign of Sultán Sikandar say that before his accession to the throne he was called Nizám Khán, and that he was remarkable for his beauty, which was unsurpassed, and that whoever looked at him yielded his heart captive. Shaikh Hasan, grandson of the Shaikh Abú Lálá, whose memory is revered in Raprí, was captivated by his appearance. One day of winter, when Prince Nizám Khán was sitting in his private chamber, Shaikh Hasan was seized with a desire of beholding him, and found no difficulty in reaching him on account of the respect *in which men of his pure mode of life are held.* (N.B.—Il Musannif has been in Turkey and has also perused the Anglo-Hibernian history of a certain Bishop of Clogher, still to be found in the records of the Diocese of Armagh, so he italicises that.)

When Sultán Sikandar, surprised at his intrusion, asked how he dared to enter without due permission, the Shaikh answered, "You know best how and why I came!" "You consider yourself fond of me?" replied the Prince. "I am unable to be otherwise," said the Shaikh.

"Come forward," said Nizám Khán, and when the Shaikh obeyed, he pressed his unresisting head towards the ardent charcoal in the stove before him.

Whilst this was going on, entered Mubárak Khán Loháni, who wondered at the sight, and said, "Oh! man that fearest not God, what are you doing? Shaikh Hasan has suffered no injury from the fire; tremble, lest you yourself should. You ought to be thankful that he should admire you, and that you should be pleasing in the sight of so holy a man. If you would obtain felicity in this world and the next, obey him."

Prince Nizám Khan then withdrew his hand from the Shaikh's neck, and everyone saw that, notwithstanding the dreadful heat of the fire, neither the face nor hair of the Shaikh had been injured. In spite of all this, the obdurate Sultán ordered the Shaikh to be chained neck and foot and cast into a dungeon. A week after they informed Sultán Sikandar that his prisoner was dancing in the bázár. When seized and brought back to the King's Tribunal, and asked how he had got loose, he said that the spirit of his grandfather had led him forth by the hand. On examining his place of confinement, his fetters were found lying on the ground. "Truly," says Il Musannif, "this Shaikh must have been the predecessor of Maskelyne and Cook."

XIX.

WHAT A ZEALOUS MUSULMÁN WAS SIKANDAR LÚDÍ!

He utterly destroyed all the temples of the infidels and left not a vestige of them. He entirely ruined the shrines of Mathurá, "the Mine of Heathenry," and turned their principal Hindú places of worship into caravanseries and colleges.

Their idols were bestowed on the fleshers to be used as meat weights, and all the Hindús were forbidden to shave their heads and beards, or to perform their customary ablutions.

Agra was his general residence, and he had re-edified it, for although it had in former ages been the state prison of Rájá Kans, of Mathurá, Mahmúd of Ghazní had almost devastated it out of existence. At length, when great Akbar ruled, it became the seat of Government of the Empire of Dehlí, and one of the chief cities of Hindústán.

XX.

HOW SULTÁN SIKANDAR DEALT WITH "TREASURE TROVE."

A person digging in the district of Sambhal lighted upon an earthen jar containing about 5,000 gold mohurs, and the Governor of that district took it forcibly from him; but when this reached the King's ears, he ordered the money to be restored to the finder.

"But," said his adviser, Miyán Kásim, "the sum is too large for a man of his position." "Oh, fool!" replied the angry monarch, "He who has given it to him would not have done so had he been unworthy of it. All men are God's servants, and He knows who is worthy and who is not." So all the gold was given back.

In the same way, a husbandman who was ploughing a field at Ajodhan, belonging to the holy Shaikh Muhammad, turned up a very large block of stone, and informed the Shaikh of the discovery. Underneath the stone was a well which was found to be full of treasure, which the Shaikh caused to be carried to his own dwelling. Some of the golden plates and vessels bore the seal of Sultán Sikandar Zú-l-Karnain (Alexander of "the Two Horns," or "the Great").

Alí Khán, the ruler of Lahore and Deobálpúr, demanded its surrender, and, when the Shaikh declined to comply, reported the matter to the Sultán, who told the Shaikh "that, as they had both an account to render to the most high God, the owner of the world, who gives to whomsoever he will, he might keep the treasure trove."

Ahmad Yádgár, in relating this anecdote, remarks, "God be praised for endowing the Sultán with such a generous spirit. *In these days, if anybody were to find a few copper coins, our rulers would immediately pull down his house to examine every nook and corner for more."*

Autres temps, autres mœurs, says Il Musannif.

XXI.

A DYING AND, CONSEQUENTLY, REPENTANT MONARCH.

Il Musannif recollects an old saying which told how "when His Satanic Majesty was unwell he became piously disposed," and this was somewhat the case with Alexander of Lúdí when he was afflicted with bronchitis. So he asked Shaikh Ládan Dánishmand (the "Artful One" whom we have had occasion to mention in another episode) what he was to do for his sins of omission of prayer and fasting, for cutting off his beard (that venerated appendage of all true sons of Islám), for indulging in strong drinks, and for cutting off men's noses and ears, an amusement the Sultán had been much given to.

So the worthy apostle whom he had taken into his counsels laid down as an irrefragable decree, that in order to preserve himself from the penalties which awaited him in the next world, and to make suitable atonement for the before-named iniquities, it would be indispensable to bestow on the pious and holy 'Ulamá, or Priests (who were of the Shaikh's own kidney), all the gold that did not strictly belong to the Exchequer.

Then the reserved funds which the Sultán had set apart out of the gifts of neighbouring princes were handed over to the 'Ulamá, who, as our author, Abdu-llah, quietly and sagely observes, "all began to praise and extol the virtues of the Sultán who had so richly lined their holy pockets."

Sultán Sikandar became more feeble every day, but his zeal stimulated him to discharge his duties as a sovereign, until his illness arrived at such a pitch that his throat would allow him neither to swallow food nor drink, and until the passage of his breath was stopped. He died on a Sunday, being the 7th day of Zí-l-Ka'da, in the year of the Departure from Mecca 923, after having sat on the throne twenty-eight years and five months.

XXII.

SULTÁN KUTBU-D-DÍN WA DUNYÁ, "THE POLE-STAR OF EARTH AND OF RELIGION."

WHEN the head of the base Malik Káfúr had been severed from his body during the night by certain officers, Mubárak was released from the captivity in which that murderous traitor had detained him; he was raised to the throne under the title of Kutbu-d-Dín wa Dunyá, and the first proceeding of this pole-star of earth and religion was, with true Hindustání gratitude, to slaughter those who had procured his elevation by the murder of his mortal foe Káfúr. But he made much amends for this, perhaps, necessary precaution in the land of Hind, by releasing the hosts of political prisoners who had been immured by the late savage monarch 'Alá-ud-Dín, and he sweetened the troops and nobles by large gratuities and presents. Heavy and oppressive tributes were lightened; extortion, beating, fetters, and blows were set aside in revenue matters. The annalist of Sultán Kutbu-d-Dín takes great notice of this rare instance of Oriental Imperial clemency, and well might he (who wrote of the year of our Lord 1317) when within these last score years Il Musannif has personally witnessed the most disgusting cruelty commonly practised for the purpose of extortion within the territories of that king of kings, Násiru-d-Dín, the highly civilized and Europeanized Sháh of Persia, who was only a few years ago the honoured, but by no means honourable, guest of our own Sovereign.

As, when the prim severity of the Puritan Commonwealth had worn out the patience of the English, and so inclined them to adopt the other extreme that the very Ironsides of Oliver became, according to Samuel Pepys, "deboshed" rascals, so did the change from the previously stern *régime* of Sultán 'Alá-ud-Dín to the easy-going and sensual career of his successor, cause reaction amongst the folk of Hindústán. All the old spydom and stringent ordinances fell into abeyance,— the Sultán was night and day a careless debauchee and free-liver, and the people followed his example.

Boys, good-looking eunuchs, and beauteous damsels rose so in the market that scarcely any were obtainable except for fabulous sums. The Multání wine-sellers sold their liquors openly at their own price, and cheated and fleeced the people. Bribery and malversation were not long in making their appearance, and gorgeous raiment was to be seen everywhere, since the abolition of the sumptuary laws of 'Alá-ud-Dín.

Murdered at last in his palace, through the treachery of Khusrú, his throne was occupied by an ungrateful usurper who had done the deed, with the co-operation of the Parwárís and Hindús, and who styled himself King Násiru-d-Dín.

No sooner had this traitor begun his reign than he remorselessly murdered every adherent of the late Sultán, and gave their wives and children to his own low caste Parwárís. Jáhamjá, the murderer of Kutbu-d-Dín was adorned with inestimable jewels; and horrid Parwárís sported in the royal harem. Khusrú forcibly espoused the wife of the late Sultán; and the Parwárís, having gained the upper hand, took to themselves the wives and handmaids of the nobles and great men.

Copies of the Holy Kurán were used as seats, and idols were set up in the mosques. Much must it have pained the pious Muhammadan scribe to recount these atrocities of the Hindú race, who, after all, were merely retaliating even greater injuries of the past on their quondam oppressors.

But retribution was at hand, for Ghází Malik, who was at that time lord of Deobálpúr, and a sturdy soldier who had long kept the frontier against the infidel hordes of the Mugháls, routed the troops of Khusrú near Daliyá, and then joined battle with the usurper at Indarput. The victory was with Ghází Khán, and his captured rival was summarily beheaded on the field of battle, much as our own King Henry VII. shortened Richard Plantagenet's adherent Catesby, in Leicester, the day after the battle of Bosworth Field.

Then the chiefs and nobles said to the conqueror, "Thou, O Ghází Malik, hast long been a barrier to the Mugháls, and hast foiled them in their attempts to invade this land of Hind, and thou hast now freed us from the yoke of the Hindús and Parwárís, and avenged our benefactors! All here present know no one but thee who is worthy of royalty." So they hailed him with general acclaim as their Sovereign, under the title of Sultánu-l-Ghází Ghiyásu-d-dunyá wa dín Tughluk Sháhu-s-Sultán.

XXIII.

HOW A VERY ARTFUL AND SAINTLY MAN "BESTED" KHÁN JAHÁN LÚDÍ.

One day, Miyán Ládan Dánishmand (or the "knowing one") went to the generous Khán Jahán, and said that he wished to eat "khichrí," and that as he had not the means of having that very Hindú and not unsavoury comestible prepared in time, he had come to "the chief of the world," in whose opulent mansion he felt sure he should find some ready.

Now the Khán had no plebeian "khichrí" at hand, and offered to have some prepared. "But," remarked the "knowing one," "during the time required for its cooking, my appetite will have left me." "Well," replied the hospitable host, "whilst it is getting ready, I will send for some 'mitháís,' or sweeties, from the bázár to lull your hunger." "Very good," quoth the holy man, "tell your servant to bring the money to me, and I will tell him what to do." When the coin was brought Miyán Ládan put it in his pouch, and said he would wait for his repast of "khichrí."

He did so, and ate so copiously that he complained of a surfeit, and said that he could not expose himself to the motion of a palanquin. "Why not ride?" said Khán Jahán. "Yes," said the "artful one," "but my horse is such an equine bear, that I should be worse off on his back than in a palanquin."

So the Khán caused an easy-pacing steed to be brought for his visitor's accommodation; but as his own horse was a myth, he had no saddle, so he asked for and got one.

"Shall I keep the animal at my home, or send him back to you?" said this Hindustání Jeremy Diddler or Robert Macaire. "No; you need not send him back," replied his bountiful entertainer. "How can I do so," replied the Miyán, "when there is no groom to look after the beast, and no pulse, gúr, or ghí, to give to it?"

When all these things had been graciously accorded to him, he begged to mention that when the present saddle had been worn out, and the horse-clothing also, they would need renewal; "and," continued he, "it would save a great deal of trouble to both of us, if you would grant me a village, the revenues of which would suffice for all expenses, including the groom's wages, the food of the horse, and for its saddle, coverings, and green fodder."

So a village was given him in the pargana of Badáún, and the "knowing one" departed, blessing his stars that there was still such open-handed fools on earth as Khán Jahán Lúdí, and forgetting to pay even his pálkí bearers, with whom his host had to settle.

XXIV.

THE RED REIGN OF MUHAMMAD TUGHLUK.

A SAVAGE and blood-thirsty bigot, yet one who opened his hand freely to the necessitous, was Sultán Abú-l-Mujáhid Muhammad Sháh.

Outside his palace at Dehlí sat his executioners on platforms, ready to slay at their master's nod. The victims were put to death at the door of the hall of audience, and their corpses were left there to taint the surrounding atmosphere for three successive days; rarely were these ghastly evidences of his cruelty wanting, and once a rider's horse shied from a white heap on the ground, which his companions told him was the trunk of a man cut into three pieces.

No distinction did he make between small errors and heinous crimes, and neither the learned, the religious, nor the noble found mercy at his hands. Daily a sad procession of hundreds of unfortunates were brought manacled before him. Some he slew, others he tortured, and a cruel beating was the least of his punishments. Friday alone was a day of respite. "God preserve us from evil," well says the chronicler of this atrocious tyranny.

He was guilty of the blood of his own brother, Mas'úd Khán, who, from fear of the torture which the Sultán invariably inflicted on all who denied his accusations, had owned to intended rebellion. The mother of this victim had been stoned two years previously on a trumped up charge of debauchery.

On one occasion, having ordered an expedition to be sent against the Hindús of the mountains, many of the soldiers remained behind; when the Sultán heard this he was exceedingly wroth, and the three hundred deserters were butchered in cold blood.

Wearied of his oppression, the people of Dehlí took to casting into his hall of audience anonymous letters filled with insults to the King; so he set his mind on the ruin of Dehlí, and forced its inhabitants to emigrate *en masse* to Daulatábád.

Woe to him who should be found within the precincts of the Imperial city after the third day.

Two poor wretches, the one paralytic, the other blind, were found after the appointed time in the deserted town, and the ruthless Sultán caused the first to be blown from a mortar, and the second whilst being dragged behind a horse from Dehlí to Daulatábád was so beaten to pieces on the way that only one of his legs reached the latter place.

Seated on the roof of his palace, this Indian Nero whilst contemplating the deserted city, so lately full of life and noisy with traffic, dared to say that his heart was now satisfied and his feelings appeased.

Even in after days when he repented him of the evil he had done, and strove to repeople Dehlí with the inhabitants of other places, the attempt succeeded but partially; so vast was the area of the city, that the new comers could but occupy a small portion of it.

When the Sultán's valiant nephew, Bahá-ud-din Gushtasp, refused to take the oath of allegiance to him, and was routed by the Imperial troops, he sought refuge with the Hindú chief of Kambila in the mountains, who seeing himself surrounded by the troops of Muhammad Sháh, and destitute of food, resolved to die rather than fall into the hands of the tyrant of Delhí!

First, however, the noble Rájpút, mindful of the sacred duties of hospitality, sent his guest to the safer guardianship of another Hindú Rájá; then he commanded a great fire to be prepared and lighted, in which he burned his furniture and goods; then turning to his wives and daughters, he told them that he was about to die, and that such of them as would follow his example, might do the same.

Then, with that devotion so commonly found amongst Hindú women in page after page of the ancient annals of Hind, all the ladies, after performing ablutions, and rubbing their bodies with the scented wood of the sandal, kissed the ground at their lord's feet, and cast themselves one after another on the burning pile. Nor was this fearsome holocaust confined to the Rájá's family alone; for the wives of his nobles, ministers, and chief men, also, imolated themselves in like fashion.

Then the Rájá, having rubbed himself also with

sandal, took his weapons, but abstained from putting on his breastplate, in order to expose himself to a speedy and assured death; he then led his band of devoted heroes against the overwhelming forces of the Sultán, and they almost all fell.

Strange to relate that the Red King for once showed some small degree of magnanimity, for eleven of the Rájá's sons having survived the battle, and having been forcibly brought within the fold of Islám, the Sultán's admiration of their father's desperate valour caused him to ennoble them, and one was seen in after days in the palace of Dehlí, under the name of Abú Muslim, who was so trusted by the suspicious tyrant that he gave into his charge the ring with which the vessel containing his own drinking water was sealed. No greater proof of confidence could have been given by the ruler of a land where poison was in habitual use, either to rid oneself of a suspected enemy, or to extirpate a tyrant.

Poor Bahá-ud-dín found no such staunch and thorough friend as he of Kambila in the pusillanimous Hindú Ráí to whom he had fled for a second refuge; for when the latter beheld the approach of the Dehlí troops, he meanly surrendered his guest into the hands of his arch-enemy.

With his legs manacled, and his arms bound to his neck, the unhappy prince was by his own uncle's command haled before the women of the zanána, who, although of his own blood, spat upon and reviled him.

Then, horrible to relate, he was flayed alive, and whilst his skin was stuffed with straw, his flesh was cooked with rice, and forced down the throats of his wife and children. What remained of this enforced cannibal repast, was, it is said, placed before the elephants, and spurned by those noble quadrupeds.

As King Muhammad had previously treated Bahádin Búra, the defeated King of Bengal, in like fashion, he commanded his stuffed skin, together with that of Bahá-ud-dín, to be exhibited throughout all the provinces of his dominions, as tangible proofs of his power and severity; but Kishlú Khán, the Governor of Sindh, caused the disgusting relics to receive Muhammadan burial.

This was more than sufficient to exasperate the tyrant, who, however, in the contest which ensued, showed no small capacity as a general, and Kishlú Khán being slain in battle, his head was suspended above the door of the palace which he had inhabited as Governor of Multán.

Retribution, however, sometimes overcame this man of blood, for when retiring from an expedition through the Himálayas against China, before an unexpected and powerful Chinese army, owing to the fatal effects of the rainy season on his soldiers and baggage-animals, the Hindús of the hills harassed his retreat with such vigour, that they almost annihilated an army which had once numbered 100,000 of his best and bravest.

"When," says the historian of these events, "the infidels found that the Musulmáns were retreating, they waited for them in the gorges of the mountains, and occupied the defiles in their front. They cut down great trees, and these they cast from the precipices, down which they fell, crushing all with whom they came in contact."

The greater part of the fighting-men and camp-followers perished, the rest were made prisoners. The Hindús seized the treasures, merchandize, horses, and arms, and of all the Musulmáns but three men of note escaped; these were the Commander Nakbia, Badru-d-dín Málik Sháh, and another.

Peace he was fain to make with the indomitable highlanders, who had made mince-meat of his power, and only a nominal tribute was conceded to him by them.

The elephants used by this amiable monarch to execute his savage decrees, had their tusks covered with sharpened steel, which was fashioned as is the coulter of a plough; the acute brutes were trained to wind their trunks round their prostrate victims, then to hurl them into the air, catch them on one of their armed teeth, and finally crush them beneath their ponderous feet.

Then to vary his amusements, the obedient animal, by his command, either tore the defunct carcase into shreds with his steely tusks, or left it to be flayed.

Gloating over many such a spectacle often sat this lord of Hind.

When Aínu-l-Mulk rebelled and was captured, he was buffeted and spat upon by the sycophants of the Court; but, wonderful to relate, the Sultán forgave him in the end.

He lost the greater part of his army in a bootless expedition to Malabar, and was forced by the pestilence to hasten back to Daulatábád. Famine added to the miseries of the land, and so terrible was the dearth that three women were seen cutting up and eating the skin of a horse which had been dead some months. Hides were cooked and sold publicly in the markets. When bullocks were slaughtered, their blood was instantly and eagerly lapped up by the famished crowd.

The whole life of this monarch was spent in pursuing visionary schemes which never met with success, and which made his reign the most calamitous that had ever been known in Hindústán.

Once he was prudent, when he bought the retreat of the Mughál hordes of Taimúrshín Khán which had begun to ravage the Panjáb, but it was not long before he planned the conquest of Persia, and to that end raised a prodigious army, which, when want of pay caused it to disband, carried ruin and rapine everywhere.

Of his Chinese expedition and its miserable termination we have already written; but hearing tell of the paper-money of China, he introduced the same system, in the shape of copper tokens, into his own dominions. His notorious insolvency and the instability of his authority destroyed the credit of this spurious coinage from the outset; foreigners would have nothing to say to the new issue; natives, although threatened with pains and penalties, evaded their acceptance; trade came to a dead halt; and although to superficial observers the payment of the royal responsibilities with these scraps of copper had been advantageous to him, the poverty of his subjects left his Exchequer vacant, and his last state became worse than his first.

Pressed by necessity, his extortions knew no bounds, until peaceable husbandmen left their fields and became highway robbers in self-defence. Towns were left without an inhabitant.

The furious ruffian then organized general "battues," after the fashion of the hunts in Germany at the present day; a circle of armed men enclosed the doomed district, and gradually closed to the centre, slaughtering like wild beasts all who crossed their path. At one fell swoop he massacred all the inhabitants of the grand old city of Kanauj.

The Afghans raided freely in the Panjáb; the Gakkars seized Lahore and ruined that province. The Rájás of the Karnatik and of Telingana recovered an independence, which they maintained against their Musulmán opponents until the days of Aurangzeb; many other rebels were there to harass the ferocious King, who showed unceasing activity and energy in suppressing them, until, when in Sindh, he was seized with sudden illness, and died in the city of Thattá, leaving only the reputation of a furious and sanguinary tyrant behind; one whose great talents might have rendered him the marvel of his age, but who, although the Muhammadan dominions he inherited eastward of the Indus were more extensive than those owned by any of his predecessors, caused the secession of many provinces, which were not reannexed to the Empire of Dehlí until the days of the perfidious and unscrupulous "Throne Adorner," we mean Aurangzeb.

Insurrection followed upon insurrection throughout the realm of Sultán Muhammad. Once he questioned his friend and historian, the poet, Ziá-ud-dín Barní, as to the advisability of severity in order to suppress these revolts; and when the latter replied that when disaffection had rooted itself in the minds of the people it could only be extirpated by tearing out the very vitals of the State, and that experience should, by this time, have taught the King that nothing was to be hoped from extreme punishment, Muhammad replied in these words, in answer:—

"In these days many wicked and turbulent men are to be found, and the punishments which you mention as having been ordained by the great Jamshíd were only suited to the earlier ages of the world. I visit my foes with chastisement upon the suspicion or presumption of treacherous designs, and punish the most trifling act of contumacy with death. This I will do until I die, or until the people act honestly, and give up rebellion. I have no such 'Wazír' as could make rules which would obviate my shedding blood."

Obdurate to the last, he slacked not in his pursuit of the rebel Taghí, who had fled to Thattá, in Sindh, and taken refuge with the "Jám" of that place; although fever- and even death-stricken, he paused not in his lust of vengeance.

Crossing the great river Indus, and marching along its banks, a surfeit of fish at the close of the fast of Muharram, which he always observed with fanatical rigidity, caused so great an increase of his malady, that he was placed in a boat, and conveyed down the stream to within fourteen kos of Thattá, where he was conquered by death on the 21st day of Muharram, in the year 752 of the Hijreh (1350 A.D.).

Then, although their tyrant-ruler had ceased to live, and was, in Farishta's language, "shut up in the dark dungeon of the grave," his army was in a pitiful plight. Encumbered with women, children, and baggage in the midst of an enemy's country, and that country the burning and arid land of Sindh, they looked on the decease of the Sultán as the forerunner of their own destruction, and despair of ever beholding their homes again saddened every heart.

Fortunately for their welfare, a preserver was amongst them in the person of Fírúz, the favourite nephew of the late monarch, who had named him as his successor, to his nobles, when he felt death to be at hand. The Mughál mercenaries, who were without the camp with their general Alti, stirred up by their own compatriot Amír Nauroz, who deserted to them during the night, bringing him a large body of the Imperial troops who were under his command, determined to seize this favourable opportunity of pillaging the treasures of the late Emperor, and returning laden with the spoil to their native steppes. On the following morning, aided by the confusion and anarchy which pervaded the Royal Camp, they made a sudden incursion into it, and carried away many camel-loads of treasure, but afterwards were severely defeated by Sultán Fírúz, as we have related in our notice of that amiable and munificent sovereign.

The renowned traveller from Tangiers, Ibn Batúta, had a narrow escape from the hands of the implacable tyrant Muhammad, although at first treated with the utmost liberality and consideration.

Received by the Queen-mother during the Sultán's absence, on his arrival in Dehlí, he was decked with magnificent robes, two thousand dínárs were bestowed on him, and a house appointed as his residence. On the Sultán's return he was treated still more splendidly. He received a grant of villages worth 5,000 dínárs a year, ten female captives and a fully caparisoned horse from the King's own stables were made over to him, as also a further sum of 5,000 dínárs. He was created a judge in Dehlí, with a salary of 12,000 dínárs annually, and allowed to draw the first year in advance.

His good fortune seemed endless, for another largesse of 12,000 dínárs came to his lot, minus *soit dit en passant*, the sum of ten per cent., which had doubtless adhered to the fingers of the officials of the royal treasury.

Most extravagant of Moors, notwithstanding all these bounties, Ibn Batúta got into debt for the rather large sum of 45,000 dínárs; this bill was, however, settled by King Muhammad, to whom the acute "Maghrabí" recited an Arabic poem of his own composition, relating the pecuniary troubles by which he was afflicted.

But the sword of Damocles hung above his head, and it was not long before he had unpleasant personal proof of the instability of the favour of an irresponsible despot.

We give the story in his own words, and with it we conclude our notice of this most detestable tyrant. Having fallen into disgrace for having paid visits to a certain Shaikh who was obnoxious to the King, the account of his terrors when placed under strict surveillance is not unamusing.

"The Sultán ordered four of his slaves never to lose sight of me in the audience-chamber, and when such an order is given it is very rarely that the person escapes. The first day the slaves kept watch over me was a Friday, and the Almighty inspired me to repeat these words of the Kurán, 'God is sufficient for us, and what an excellent Protector!'

"On that day I repeated this sentence 33,000 times, and I passed the night in the audience-chamber. I fasted five days in succession. Every day I read the whole of the Kurán, and broke my fasts only by drinking a little water.

"The sixth day I took some food, then I fasted four days more in succession, and I was released after the death of the Shaikh. Thanks be to the Almighty."

This so frightened Ibn Batúta that he lost no time in resigning his office, and avoiding the dangerous neighbourhood of "the Red King." Muhammad, however, appears to have forgiven his imprudence in the matter of the Shaikh, for he shortly afterwards sent him as his ambassador to the Emperor of China.

XXV.

THE GOOD TIMES OF FÍRÚZ THE KING.

In the midst of the anarchy, bloodshed, treachery, and desolation which stain almost every page of the annals of Hind, there are some bright spots, and we regard the reign of Fírúz Tughluk as one of these.

Little marked by brilliant exploits or successful warfare, it was devoted to the happiness of his subjects; and although 500 years have elapsed since his death, no small number of his many public works remain to greet the eye of the traveller.

Lands he assigned for the maintenance of 50 dams across rivers to promote irrigation, of 40 mosques, 30 colleges, 100 caravanseries, 30 reservoirs, 100 hospitals, 100 public baths, and 150 bridges, besides many pleasure-houses and other edifices.

But the chief monument now existing of this beneficent monarch, the worthy precursor of Akbar, and which still sheds fertility around, is the canal which bears his name, and which starts from where the Jamna leaves the mountains and passes by Kamál to Hansí and Hisár and the river Gágar.

As was invariably the case in that land of discord, it was neglected after the death of Sháh Fírúz, and the branch of it which reached to the Satlaj, is of use no longer; that portion of it which has been restored by the British Government, now turns corn, oil, and sugar mills; the wood hewn in the mountains floats down its stream for some 200 miles, and it is even navigable by boats; but its great object has been that irrigation which made the pastoral habits of the surrounding country give way to the tillers of the soil.

Born A.D. 1309, he was the son of the Muhammadan Lord of Deobálpúr, by the beautiful and accomplished daughter of the high-caste Hindú Ráná Mal Bhattí.

The courtship of his parents was no milk-and-water wooing, and, in fact, savoured greatly of coercion; for when the Ráná treated the Governor Tughluk's proposal of a matrimonial alliance with his own brother, Sipáh-Sálár, or "Commander-in-Chief," Rajab, with considerable contumely, the incensed Muhammadan chief, knowing very well that it would not be forthcoming, demanded with threats the entire amount of the yearly revenue due by the Ráná in specie, and for three days the Hindús were subjected to every species of ignominy and maltreatment.

But let the annalist, Shams-i-Siráj 'Afíf, relate the sequel in his own words.

"The mother of Ráná Mal seeing the extremities and hardship to which her people were rendered by the severity of Tughluk Sháh, proceeded, at the time of evening-prayer, to the house of her son, weeping and tearing her hair. Now it so happened that Ráná Mal's daughter, the future mother of Fírúz Sháh, was in the court-yard. When that fortunate damsel heard the wailing and crying of the Ráná's mother, she inquired what was the cause of her grief; and the dame replied, 'I am weeping on your account, for it is through you that Tughluk Sháh is weighing so heavily on the people of this land.' Then the noble and high-spirited girl exclaimed, 'If the surrender of me will deliver the people from such misery, comply instantly with the demand, and send me to him; consider then that the Mughals have carried off one of your daughters.'

"The old lady went and told the Ráná of his daughter's resolution, and he gave his assent; a messenger was sent to Tughluk Sháh, and the damsel herself brought to Deobálpúr, where she espoused the Sipáh-Salár.

"After the lapse of a few years she gave birth to Fírúz Sháh, in a most auspicious hour, and Tughluk Sháh distributed his bounty on all sides in token of his joy."

Losing his father at the early age of seven, he was adopted and educated by his uncle Tughluk, and when the latter mounted the throne as Muhammad Sháh, Fírúz was his constant companion, and his uncle the steadfast friend and instructor of the youth in the duties of that royalty to which he wished him to succeed.

When the breath left his uncle's body, Fírúz had attained the ripe age of forty-five, and at that time the Imperial camp lay at Thattá, in the torrid land of Sindh. Anarchy had arisen in consequence of the Sultán's decease, and the army was far away from Dehlí; the robber Mugháls took advantage of the confusion to plunder the baggage-train, and at last, seeing no hope of a safe return to their native land, unless guided by a skilful and trusty leader, they unanimously selected Fírúz.

After the fashion of the bishops of our own day who give forth their *Nolo episcoparis* without the slightest intention of persisting in a permanent refusal, Fírúz affected unwillingness to assume the royal diadem, and spoke of ending his days at Mecca, that refuge of Indian Wolseys and disinherited princes and nobles in the ancient days of Hind, and much akin to holy Kerbela, near Baghdád, where those who have fallen into the bad graces of Sháh Násiru-d-din of Irán, either fly or are banished to.

Giving, however, at length, an apparently reluctant assent to the pressing solicitations of the princes, judges, doctors, and officials, but especially appearing to be influenced by the entreaties of the holy Shaikhs, he allowed himself to be crowned and invested with the robes of sovereignty, which he put on over the garments of mourning for his uncle.

"No!" said the new King to his amírs, "although

in compliance with your counsels I have assumed the royal robes, I cannot throw off the garb of sorrow which I wear for Sultán Muhammad, my lord, my teacher, my guide, and my benefactor."

Thus he rode forth on an elephant, the drums were exultingly beaten, and the heralds and attendants shouted.

This event took place on the 23rd day of March A.D. 1351, corresponding to the 24th of Muharram, in the year of the Departure of the Prophet from Mecca 752.

He began his reign by thoroughly beating the Mughâls, who had been so troublesome, and then marched on to Dehlí, to find that the late sovereign's deputy there, Khwájá-i-Jahán, had installed a son of the late Muhammad in the royal seat. Vainly did the Khwájá endeavour to bring the amírs, the troops, and the people to his views; for although their fingers clutched his gifts, their hearts were with King Fírúz.

So Fírúz moved onwards, and the Khwájá was greatly discomfited when great and small poured out from the city to welcome the man they loved; and when he heard that the King, as he came along, had met nought but joyous faces and willing friends, amongst whom was the great and powerful noble, Kiwámu-l-Mulk, the Kháir-i-Jahán, or "Lord of the World," who had forced his way out of Dehlí sword in hand.

So Khwájá Jahán, who was a white-haired old man of eighty, made up his mind to cast himself on the clemency of one whom in the past he had been wont to style "his son."

Accordingly, he made his way to Fathábád, where a son had just been born to the Sultán, and presented himself before his former friend, without his turban, with a chain round his neck, and a naked sword fastened round his throat; then the Sultán had compassion on him, and, after causing his turban to be replaced on his head, he sent him in his own palanquin to a spot where they might conveniently hold an interview.

But, although the sovereign had forgiven, the chief nobles were obstinately bent on the destruction of the Khwájá, who, when on his road to his place of retirement at Sámána, was overtaken by his enemy Shír Khán.

Looking at the executioner who accompanied this chieftain, and who had been his friend, he asked to see his weapon; he then told the man of blood to perform his ablutions, say his prayers, and then use his sword.

"When he had complied," says the chronicler, "the Khwájá bound his head to his prayer-carpet, and while the name of God was on his lips, his head was severed from his body."

Not a good beginning to a reign, this outpouring of

the blood of an aged man and an old friend; but Sultán Fírúz had done his utmost to prevent the catastrophe, and as he was not yet firmly established, he was still at the mercy of his turbulent nobility.

On the entry of the King into Dehlí, great was the rejoicing, and magnificent the bounty and festivities, which lasted for the space of one-and-twenty days.

Notwithstanding that the people of Dehlí had to a great extent been accomplices of the treason of Khwájá Jahán, he forgave the sums which had been lent them after the days of the great famine by the late Sultán Muhammad, for the purpose of restoring their lands and villages which had fallen into ruin, and generously cancelled the records of their debts.

During his reign of forty years, the revenues of Dehlí amounted to 67,500,000 "tankas." He distributed villages and lands amongst his followers, and during all that time "not one leaf was shaken in the palace of sovereignty. If an officer in his army died he was succeeded by his son, or by his son-in-law in the absence of the former, even by a slave, or by his wives if there were no male descendants."

It is to be presumed, then, that some of his regiments had lady-colonels, who, although they drew the emoluments of their rank, rarely appeared on parade, and seldom, or never, faced the horrors of actual warfare.

No exactions were allowed beyond the payment of the legal Government dues; not a doit was taken from the peasant, who became wealthy and contented. If the account of the historian, Shams-i-Siráj 'Afíf, be true, and we see no reason for doubting its veracity, "the houses of the 'raiyats' were filled with grain, horses, and furniture; everyone had abundance of gold and silver; no woman was without her ornaments, and no house was wanting in excellent beds and couches. Wealth abounded, and the whole realm of Dehlí was blessed with the bounties of the Almighty."

But there was treason in the very bosom of the household of the King, for his first cousin, Khudáwand-záda, the daughter of Tughluk Sháh, and wife of Khusrú Malik, who had been bitterly incensed at his accession to the throne, and at the supersession of her own son, sought to destroy him.

In her palace, which adjoined that of Fírúz, she posted some armed men in two lateral chambers to the apartment in which she received the weekly visits which her royal cousin never failed to pay her after having performed his devotions at the mosque each Friday.

Warned by signs made by the son of Khudáwand-záda by another husband than the base-born Malik Khusrú, the Sultán evaded the peril, and, after convicting his relative of the plot against his life, banished and pensioned her, whilst he bestowed the highest honours of the court on the young relation, Dáwar Malik, who had given him such timely warning, although he had personally been the greatest sufferer by the enthronement of Sháh Fírúz.

We leave aside his wars in Bengal and the Dakhin, and his failure against the Prince of Sindh, preferring rather to dwell on the enlightened spirit of his regulations, the extent and utility of his public works, and on his many deeds of benevolence.

Once Malik Isháḳ, the son of 'Imádu-l-Mulk, reported to Sháh Fírúz that it would be for the benefit of the service should the old and enfeebled soldiers be replaced by younger and more vigorous ones. Now 'Imádu-l-Mulk held high office in the State, and the Sháh appearing to agree with Malik Isháḳ, told him first to turn out his own father as a preliminary to the dismissal of other old servants, and added these kindly words when he saw how suddenly his officious adviser had been taken aback by this unexpectedly prompt compliance with his representation:

"If I remove the old and inefficient men, and appoint their sons or strangers in their stead, the poor old fellows will fall into distress in their age. This I do not approve of, and will never encourage disobedience in children; their sons, if they succeed, may prove undutiful and break the hearts of their parents by their neglect. Order that the son shall become the deputy of his old and incapable father, and that he shall support the veteran in his home."

Then Sultán Fíruz bore away the stone columns of the older times of Hindúism, from Khizrábád and Mírat, and set them up in his palace in the city of Fírúzábád, which he had founded. "They had been," says the pious and veracious son of Islám from whom we derive our information, 'the sticks of the accursed infidel Bhím, who used them to keep his cattle together, and whose ordinary daily allowance of food was seldom less than a hundred 'mans' a day." A good appetite had this benighted heathen.

Other obelisks were also transferred to Dehlí and its vicinity; and when the Sháh hunted, he always slew the beasts of prey, such as the tiger and the wolf, before pursuing more inoffensive game.

Save and excepting his severe intolerance to those of the Hindú religion, whose temples of recent date he destroyed, and replaced by mosques, he was the well-wisher of all his subjects. When he had built edifices of every kind for the common weal, he turned his attention to the workmen and artificers who were out of employ, and provided for them amongst his nobles. Vast were his thirty-six royal establishments from his elephant, horse, and camel-stables, down to the kitchen and wardrobe.

When a feudatory came to Court, his accounts were audited at the Treasury, and a strict account of them rendered to the Court. When some of the officials of his mint had been accused of debasing the coinage of his realm, they were submitted to a searching investigation; and when their innocence was proved, the two false witnesses who had informed against them were sent into banishment.

Allowances were made to dowerless damsels from the Imperial Treasury, which also disbursed the cost of hospitals, physicians, and medicines, for the relief of the needy sick.

Each Friday, after devotions, gymnasts, story-tellers, and buffoons, to the number of some 3,000 gathered at the palace-gate to amuse the citizens of the four quarters of Dehlí.

Once when the good Fírúz, who was a strict religionist, in the year of our era 1374, went on pilgrimage to the tomb of Sálár Mas'úd Ghází, in the town of Bahráich, it is said that the spirit of the Saint appeared to him in a dream, stroking his own beard with his hand, as warning him of his approaching departure from the world.

Portrait-painting, as akin to the representation of idols, he strictly forbade, and metal vessels he eschewed as contravening the law of Muhammad; on stone or earthenware alone did he partake of his repasts.

Many oppressive imposts were put an end to; and now, as our space is small, and the annals of "the Romantic Land of Hind" infinite, before depicting the somewhat sorry end of so generally good and just a Sovereign, we are fain to give one sad instance of how far the unsparing tenets of the religion which owed its origin to the camel-driver of Mecca, could pervert the feelings of one whose nature habitually overflowed with the cream of human kindness.

It had been reported to the Sultán that an old Bráhman of Dehlí persisted in publicly performing idol-worship in his own house, and that many Musulmáns and Hindús joined in his devotions; the Bráhman was also accused of having perverted Muhammadan women to infidelity. When carried before the King at Fírúzábád, and ordered by the doctors of the law there assembled either to accept the creed of Islám or to die by fire, he stubbornly refused compliance.

Then a pile of faggots was built up at the gate of the Darbár, and the Bráhman and the painted tablet which he worshipped were cast upon it; one cry only did the poor wretch utter, when the flames first reached his feet, but it was soon silenced by the blazing wood.

Something like this happened some two centuries after in Smithfield, and other parts of this Christian island, in the days of grim Mary Tudor and her Mephistopheles of a husband, King Philip of Spain.

So deeply did the King grieve for the evil deeds of his late uncle Muhammad, who, although a firm friend and loving relative to him personally, had been so mercilessly tyrannical to others, that he did his utmost to atone for the miseries inflicted on so many during the preceding reign, and thus he relates in what manner he fulfilled this errand of mercy :—

"Under the guidance of the Almighty, I arranged that the heirs of those persons who had been slain by my late lord and patron, Sultán Muhammad Sháh, and those who had been deprived of a limb, nose, eye, hand, or foot, should be reconciled to the late Sultán, and be appeased with gifts, so that they executed deeds declaring their satisfaction. These deeds were put into a chest, which was placed in the Dáru-l-amán, at the head of the tomb of the late Sultán, in the hope that God, in His great clemency, would show mercy to my late friend and patron, and make those persons feel reconciled to him."

"Another instance of Divine guidance was this :— Villages, lands, and ancient patrimonies of every kind had been wrested from the hands of their owners in former reigns, and had been brought under the Exchequer. I directed that every one who had a claim to property should bring it forward in the law-court, and, upon establishing his title, the village, land, or property should be restored to him. By God's grace I was impelled to this good action, and men obtained their just rights."

But the good King was well stricken in years, and at length, to the sorrow of his people, when he attained his eighty-seventh year (A.D. 1385), his increasing infirmities deprived him of that energy which he had hitherto brought in all matters of government, and his "wazír" Jahán gradually became omnipotent in the realm.

Relying on the influence he had attained, and eager to insure its permanency, this base minister persuaded his aged master that his life was in peril at the hands of his own son, Prince Násiru-d-dín, the heir-apparent to the throne.

Men were sent to arrest the Prince, but he received timely warning, gathered armed adherents together, and fortified himself in his own palace. Thus he remained for some days; but at length he contrived to introduce himself, clad in complete armour, secretly into the seraglio.

When the affrighted women, in fear of so unexpected and warlike an apparition, hastened to alarm the Sultán concerning the supposed treasonable designs of his offspring, the latter followed them into his father's presence, and, falling at his feet, begged for death rather than to be allowed to remain under the burthen of such unjust and groundless suspicions.

Much moved, the weeping monarch clasped Násiru-d-dín in his arms, and gave him all power over the false witness Jahán.

No time was lost in executing the royal decree, and the house of the perfidious and aspiring minister was surrounded by 12,000 horse.

As courageous as he was devoid of every principle of honour and gratitude, Jahán charged valiantly forth amidst his assailants, and, although wounded, succeeded in effecting his escape into the land of Mewat, leaving all his wealth in the Prince's hands.

Then the old sovereign abdicated in favour of his son, whose incapacity for government and intense devotion to sensual pleasure soon became so painfully apparent that two of his cousins raised a sedition in Dehlí.

The great city became the scene of internecine civil war; terrible was the carnage, and the corpses of the slain strewed every street. Two days did the struggle endure, and on the third they bore the good old nonagenarian Fírúz out from the palace. No sooner were his well-known and well-loved form and face descried, than the affections of the troops came back to their ancient lord, and Násiru-d-dín (or Muhammad), being utterly deserted, fled in haste to the mountains of Sarmúr.

Feeling acutely his own inability to occupy longer, with efficiency, the exalted post he had held so long and so worthily, Fírúz declared his grandson Ghirásu-d-dín Tughluk monarch in his stead, and then departed from life at the great age of ninety, on the third day of Rámazán, in the year of the "Departure" 790, and in that of our Lord 1388.

XXVI.

SULTÁN RAZIYA, THE FIRST EMPRESS OF INDIA.

Now, although of the softer (?) sex, this lady was called by a *manly* title, and she was "*the Sultán,*" and not "*the Sultána,*" of Hind, as the Oriental experience of a certain Anglo-Indian civilian ought to have taught him ere he carped and cavilled at the present "Imperial" title of Victoria, the First British Empress of Hind (whom may God long preserve), and thereby showed his crass ignorance of Oriental lore.

Far be it from me (Il Musannif, to wit) to institute comparisons between past and present rulers of the Great Peninsula, but, although Minháju-s-Siráj freely admits that the fair Raziya was "a great monarch," and that she was wise, just, and generous, a benefactor to her kingdom, a dispenser of justice, the leader of her armies, and endowed *with all kingly* qualities, he cannot refrain from the ungallant remark, *that as she belonged to the wrong sex, all these virtues weighed as nothing in the balance.*

Even in the days of her father, Sa'id Shamsu-d-dín, her influence was very great, and when he had overcome strong Gwáliár, he willed his able and beautiful daughter to be his successor in preference to any of his male offspring, whose debauchery, in his opinion, unfitted them to wield the sceptre.

When, after his decease, she was raised to the throne by the general acclamation of the guards (after the fashion of the old Prætorians of Rome, or of the Janissaries of Constantinople), she rid herself of Sultán Ruknu-d-dín, who never again came forth alive from the dungeon into which she had cast him, but died in November, A.D. 1236, after having squandered and wasted his patrimony by his too profuse liberality, and by his drunkenness and abandonment of his kingly duties.

"May God pardon him!" says the pious scribe.

Il Musannif is rather inclined to think that he died no natural death, for in those far-away times a prison and a grave were strictly synonymous terms for deposed monarchy, not only in the land of Hind, but in our own sea-surrounded island, as its past history well proves.

Nizámu-l-Mulk Junaidí, the Chief Wazír of the Empire, felt repugnance for such government of petticoats, and under his banner gathered many chiefs who raised the standard of insurrection against Queen Raziya, who, unawed by the defeat of one of her chief adherents, frightened her opponents into a temporary truce, and slew those chiefs who were still recalcitrant.

Some unwise appointments caused jealousy amongst the nobles and amírs of Turkish blood, and, at last, the Queen of India, casting all Muhammadan ideas concerning the seclusion of her sex to the four winds of heaven, rode forth on an elephant in masculine garb, and veiled not her face from the common eye.

Gwáliár was taken by her officers, and she checked in person the revolt of the Governor of Lahore, but with feminine weakness she had fallen into the toils of a certain Abyssinian, Amír Jalálu-d-dín Yákút (or "the Ruby"), her infatuation for whom caused his death, and her own confinement in the fortalice of Tabar-Hind, where the chief of the place, Malik Altúniya (or, in the Turkish tongue, the "Golden King"), not only espoused her cause, but herself also.

In the meantime Mu'izzu-d-dín had usurped her place on the throne of Dehlí, and her chamberlain had been put to death, and when she and her new husband encountered their opponent they were put to flight and abandoned at Kaithal by the very few adherents who remained to them.

By Hindú hands, says Minháju-s-Siráj, they perished, after *Sultán* Raziya had governed the land of Upper Hind for the short space of three years and six months.

Sic transit gloria feminæ et reginæ.

XXVII.

HOW THE ONLY FEMALE MONARCH OF HIND CAME TO HER END.

(From another Annalist.)

When the "Sultán" Raziya had been deposed on account of her suspected intimacy with a negro, she revolted (as has been before related by Il Musannif) against her younger brother, Násiru-d-dín, who had been chosen in her stead, and when defeated she sought safety in flight, and when hunger and fatigue overcame her she begged food and drink from a field-labourer.

Hungrily devouring the leathery "chapátí" which he gave her, she fell asleep from sheer lassitude. Dressed though she was in masculine attire, the peasant who watched her repose perceived beneath her outer-coat a tunic embroidered with gold lace and precious stones; other signs showing the villain that she was of the female sex, he did not hesitate to murder her in her sleep, to strip her of her ornaments, to steal her horse, and to hide her dead body beneath the clods of the field.

But, as has often happened to malefactors of his sort, when he attempted to sell her garments, the old-clothes dealers and pawnbrokers of the period saw something crooked in the transaction, and haled him before the

Kotwál, who administered a good sound thrashing to him.

Under the pressure of the stick, the rascal not only confessed his crime, but pointed out where he had buried the unfortunate woman. Then her corpse was interred with all the rites of Islám, and a small shrine was erected over her remains, which came in after-ages to be regarded by the pilgrims from afar as a spot of extreme sanctity, on the banks of the Jamna, about a "parasang" from Dehlí.

What became of the assassin is not told us, but it is more than probable that *his* shrift was a very very short one.

XXVIII.

THE SLAYER OF HIS UNCLE.

Now Jalálu-d-dín Ghiljai was an old man of three-score and ten when he began to reign, in the 687th year after the "Departure." That he should have inaugurated his accession by the dastardly murder of the boy-son of his successor, would seem to us inexplicable in view of his after lenity to his opponents, were it not a time-honoured custom of Oriental sovereigns to blind, mutilate, or kill all those who might, from reasons of consanguinity, be brought forward subsequently to contest the possession of the throne.

Simple and jovial in his manners, he remained on the same footing of friendly familiarity with his former friends as before his elevation to the royal dignity, and his main failing was that he indulged in convivial entertainments, which, however, never exceeded the bounds of sobriety.

As the historian Farishta remarks, "Clemency is a virtue which descends from God, but the degenerate children of Hind did not deserve it, and the mild Government of Jalálu-d-dín Firúz the Second was only productive of disorder; the streets and high-ways were infested by banditti, house-breaking, robbery, murder, and every other species of villainy became a business all over the empire; insurrections broke out in every province, gangs of robbers put an end to all traffic, and the governors of the provinces sent no accounts of their revenues or administration."

This state of things so exasperated the nobles that they conspired to assassinate the Emperor, with so little secrecy that he was informed of their plans, and had them arrested whilst still hot with wine.

Causing these topers to be haled before him, he cast a sword down before them, exclaiming hotly the while, "Ah! drunken negroes, who bray and chatter, one of killing me with an arrow, another of slaying me with a sword! Is there one among you who dare lift this sword and fight it out fairly with me?"

Then one of his chief attendants played the peacemaker, and won the pardon of the culprits easily from the forgiving monarch, who even made them sit down and shared his own wine with them; a wonderful instance of clemency in vindictive Hind, where forbearance has ever been and ever will be attributed by the majority to timidity.

Whenever Jalálu-d-dín was incensed with any of his nobles, he was accustomed to threaten them with the wrath of his second son, Arkalí, who was of a most violent temperament; and when Mauláná Siráju-d-dín Sáwi, after having had the impudence to pen a bitter lampoon against him, on his subsequent repentance and appearance at court in penitent guise, with a rope round his neck, the Emperor not only embraced him and gave him a dress of honour, but enrolled him amongst his own attendants, and gave him back the village which he had forfeited through his unwise satire.

He was a bounteous patron, too, of the great poet Amír Khusrú.

Now, Sídí Mulla, a darwesh of great fame, who had come from the up-country in the time of Balban to Dehlí, was at that time notorious for his sanctity and liberality; but he prayed not in mosques, and had no servants. Where he had acquired the vast treasure which he daily and profusely expended in hospitality and gifts to every passer-by, was a mystery to the world, and rumour consequently gave him the reputation of a sorcerer. Gradually it became noised abroad that his house was a resort of the seditious of the land, and that plans had been concocted there by influential nobles and others to kill the Sultán whilst engaged in his Friday-devotions in the mosque, and to raise Sídí Mulla himself to the rank of Khalífah.

But there was a traitor, as is generally the case, in the camp of the disaffected, who had already partitioned the Empire amongst them, much as Owen Glendower, Mortimer, and Hotspur are reported to have done in the pages of our own immortal Shakspeare, and he carried tidings of the plot to the Sultán.

Dragged before their Sovereign, they persisted in strenuously denying their guilt, and as there was great evidence of their intended crime, it was resolved to endeavour to elicit a confession from them in the old ferocious way, unhappily not confined to the India of the Middle Ages alone, by the savage torments of the ordeal of fire.

But as those who were learned in the law objected to the illegality of this, some were banished and deprived of their possessions, and some were pardoned, and the chief conspirator, Kází Kasháni (evidently a Persian reprobate from Kashán), was even sent as Chief Judge to Badáún.

Sídí Mulla, whose liberality had only had for its object to win popular favour the better to carry out his ambitious schemes against the Crown, was excepted, however, from the almost general amnesty, and was brought, bound, before the palace. "Oh, darweshes," cried the King to some of these religious mendicants who were at hand, "who amongst you will give this wretch his deserts?"

One of them soon displayed his respect for the royal utterance by slashing the rebellious Mulla with the first sharp instrument at hand, a razor; but the victim might still have been spared, had not the rough and passionate Arkalí Khán made a sign from the palace to a mahaut to drive his elephant over the Mulla, who was soon trampled to death beneath the feet of the huge animal.

The historian, Ziá-ud-dín Barní, considers this a most sacreligious deed, because, although the Mulla was a traitor and a conspirator, he was a darwesh (!), whose misdeeds it was sinful to punish as severely as those of ordinary individuals, and to it he attributes the drought and famine which subsequently desolated the country.

Now the same *annalist* (Il Musannif does not dignify him with the noble name of *historian*) records in what manner the Sultán Jalálu-d-dín, after reconnoitring the strong defences of Ratambhor, and finding them impregnable with the means he then possessed, and not to be taken without sacrificing the lives of many Musulmáns, "every hair of whose heads he held to be of greater price than the possession of so important a heathen stronghold," displayed a great amount of "fox and the grapes" magnanimity. "Were I to capture the place," said the beneficent monarch, "after the fall of so many Muhammadans, the widows and orphans would rise in judgment against me, and curse me with all the bitterness of mourning despair."

So, as discretion seemed to be the better part of valour, in the face of the firm and determined Rájpúts who thronged the ramparts of Ratambhor, the Sultán withdrew to Dehlí.

Yet, in spite of this display of weakness, when 'Abdu-llah, the grandson of the "accursed" Tátár Hulákú, invaded Hind with fifteen times 10,000 of his "moss-trooper" Mugháls, the octogenarian Emperor took heart of grace and marched steadily to their rencontre.

At Bar-rám (wherever that may be, for our chronicler's locality is here much befogged) the Mughál advance-guard, which had dashed across an unnamed river, were routed with much carnage.

This led to a suspension of hostilities, and, finally, to a peace, through which many of the Mughâls remained in Hind after the departure of their chief, 'Abdu-llah, under their chief Ulghú, who espoused the daughter of Jalálu-d-dín; whilst the inferior Mughâls, who had accepted the tenets of the Kurán and renounced idolatry, were settled in those suburbs of Dehlí which were known as Kilú-gharí, Ghiyáspúr,

Indarpat and Talúká, and there they trooped with their families, and gave their national name to the new and great suburban city of Mughálpúr, where they were known as "New Musulmáns." And this came to pass in the year of the Christian era, 1292.

Minor expeditions to Mandúr and Jháín followed this campaign, and about this time 'Alá-ud-dín, the nephew and son-in-law of Jalálu-d-dín, captured the idol-gods of Bhilsa, which were trodden under foot by the True Believers at the gate of Badáún. Treated from his childhood as a favourite son, there was nothing the loving uncle could deny his relative, who was Governor of Karrah and a portion of Awadh, or Oudh.

Fired with the reports of the opulence of the land of Deogír, without the knowledge of his uncle, whom he hoodwinked as to his real object by affecting to wish to overcome the district of Chanderí, he equipped his troops with the revenues of his own governments, and marched with a scant force of less than 8,000 men to Elichpúr and Ghatilájaura, at which latter place all trace of him was lost.

Now, 'Alá-ud-dín was on bad terms with his mother-in-law, as has often been the case in other lands and amongst people who were not Muhammadans, and the Sultán's daughter, his own wife, disobeyed and scorned him, and he shunned the disgrace which a public knowledge of his derogatory position would bring on him; wherefore he determined to win a position in some remote territory, where he should cease to be the butt of feminine intrigue and duplicity.

Plunging boldly into a country as yet untrod by the feet of the children of Islám, he dispersed the forces of the Hindú Rájá of Deogír, Rám-deo, and became the possessor of much booty in treasure, elephants, and horses, when he forced his way with the armed hand into that city.

When news of this reached the aged monarch, who was then in the neighbourhood of Gwálíár, he was very glad, for he imagined that his darling nephew would joyfully lay his spoils at his feet, and he gave great entertainments and drank wine to celebrate the successes of 'Alá-ud-dín.

Relying on the fidelity of his relative, and shutting his ears to the advice of those who counselled him to beware of his nephew's ambition, he returned to Dehlí and took no steps to check the subtle and daring man who was plotting his downfall, and who merely bamboozled him by a mock affectation of fidelity and loyalty.

The too trustful senior was at length persuaded to follow his perfidious nephew to where he had posted his forces between Mánikpúr and Karrah, on the banks of the rain-swollen Ganges. The surrender of the prize-property of Deogír was the bait which 'Alá-ud-dín dangled on the point of the hook which was to catch his infatuated uncle, who came unsuspiciously with but a small retinue, and even left a portion of that whilst he crossed the river with some unarmed men.

Let Ziá-ud-din Barní relate the sequel of this tragedy.

"The Sultán reached the opposite shore before afternoon prayer, and disembarked with his few followers. 'Alá-ud-dín advanced to receive him, he and all his officers showing him due respect. When he reached the Sultán he fell at his feet, and the Sultán, treating him like a son, kissed his eyes and cheeks, stroked his beard, gave him two loving taps on the cheek, and said, 'I have brought thee up from infancy, why art thou afraid of me?' The Sultán took the hand of 'Alá-ud-dín, and at that moment the stony-hearted traitor gave the fatal signal. Muhammad Sálim of Sámána, an ill-conditioned fellow, struck at the Sultán with his sword, but missed his aim and wounded himself in the hand; a second blow, however, wounded the Emperor, who fled towards the river, crying, 'Thou villain, 'Alá-ud-dín! what hast thou done?' and Ikhtiyáru-d-dín Ibíd ran after the betrayed monarch, threw him down, cut off his head, and bore it, dripping with blood, to the graceless and ungrateful nephew, who atrociously placed it on a spear and paraded it through the camp, after which he assumed the emblems of usurped and basely acquired dominion."

But Divine retribution did not tarry long in its punishment of the assassins. The traitor, Almás Bey, met with an early death, as did others; the murderer, Sálim, the poor King's first assailant, died horribly of leprosy. The head-cutter, Ikhtiyáru-d-dín went mad, crying in his delirious ravings that the menacing spectre of the murdered monarch ever haunted him and held a naked sword above his head; and although 'Alá-ud-dín reigned successfully for years, and things prospered to his wishes, though he had wives, children, adherents, and wealth and grandeur, yet the Avenger of Blood dealt heavily with his nearest and dearest, until they were effaced from the surface of the earth.

XXIX.

THE PROSPEROUS ASSASSIN.

Some say that the wicked never prosper, but such was not the case with the murderer of his uncle and father-in-law, for one success followed another in unbroken luxuriance, victories were of every-day occurrence, and the treasury of 'Alá-ud-dín was filled to repletion.

Intoxicated with such unceasing success, his ambition enticed him into the most extravagant schemes, and although he could neither read nor write, and was bad-tempered, obstinate, and hard of heart, the world smiled on him, and Fortune stood his friend.

Two projects especially occupied his attention, and one of them was, that as God Almighty had granted to the "Blessed Prophet" "Four Friends," through whose energy the Law and Islám had been established, so God had given 'Alá-ud-dín the same number of attached companions, Ulugh Khán, Zafar Khán, Nusrat Khán, and Alp Khán,—these men who had aided and abetted him with such hearts and souls as they had in the cowardly murder of Sultán Jalálu-d-dín, and in the subsequent massacre of his adherents.

"Now, with the help of these faithful ones," quoth the aspiring usurper, "I have it in my power to set up a new belief and to force the recalcitrant to accept it, so that my name and that of my companions will remain until the Judgment-Day, like the name of the Prophet and his friends."

"Secondly," said he, "as I possess wealth, elephants, and military forces to an incalculable extent, I think of leaving the care of Dehlí to my Viceroy, and of sallying abroad, like the Conqueror Alexander, and subduing the whole habitable world."

Then, in his drinking-bouts,—for much did he love forbidden drink, and after he had assumed the vain title of a Second Alexander on his coinage,—he would boast of what he would do, until his wild schemes began to alarm his subjects.

Dropping, at length, his project of founding a new religion, by the advice of a wise counsellor, who pointed out its impossibility, and instanced the example of Janjíz Khán, who, although he had deluged so many Muhammadan lands with blood, had never succeeded in establishing Mughál institutions or creed amongst the Muslims, whilst many Mughals had entered the ranks of the Faithful, he moderated his extravagant schemes of foreign conquest, and turned his attention to the entire subjugation of Hindústán and to the defence of his north-western frontier against the raids of the Mughals.

As he marched to the siege of Ratambhor, his nephew Akat Khán, the "Wakíldár," who aspired to the throne, attacked him on the road, and the Sultán narrowly escaped, after having received two arrow wounds.

Thinking that the Sultán was dead, this worthy emulator of his uncle's former crime, rushed to the Imperial tent, and at first gained the homage of many of the chiefs, who credited the account he gave of the death of 'Alá-ud-dín.

But the wounds of the Emperor had been bandaged, and though he had lost much blood, and his arm was placed in a sling, he had nerve enough to proceed in all haste with a scanty following to the camp; and when Akat Khán heard of his return, he saddled his horse and fled, but was overtaken and beheaded, and his skull exhibited in Dehlí and in Jháín.

Dire was the chastisement of those who were proved,

or even suspected, of complicity in the deed; their property was confiscated, their families treated with the utmost rigour, and they themselves were scourged to death with an Indian "cat" of far more than *nine* tails, every tail being of *wire*.

Others were blinded "by having their eyes cut out, like the slices of a lemon," as the chronicler remarks with that unction which almost invariably marks the Hindústání writer when dealing with some outrageous act of cruelty, and whilst the siege of Ratambhor, which held out stoutly, dragged on wearily with much carnage on either side, a certain fearless and violent Hájí who had been the slave of a former Kotwál of Dehlí, rose in insurrection in that city, which at that time suffered much from the oppression and exactions of the new magistrate, Turmuzí.

Taking advantage of the great heat of the weather, which had induced most of the inhabitants, and, amongst others the Kotwál, to take their "siestas," Hájí, with some other conspirators, took the unwary officer by surprise, and after cutting off his head, proclaimed to the populace that, by a royal "farmán," which supposititious document he flourished before their eyes, he had acted thus in obedience to the Sultán's mandate.

Then he went boldly to the "Red Castle," which was so miserably made redder by the slaughter of English women and children, whose deaths were so justly avenged on the princely villains and dastards who had been the chief instigators of the massacre in 1857.

Opening the royal treasury, and showering gold profusely around, for eight days Hájí Maula remained master of Dehlí; then the brave Amír Hamídu-d-dín burst open the Ghazní gate of the town, and slew the rebel with his own hand after a desperate personal struggle.

And here we leave for awhile the affairs of "the Prosperous Assassin."

XXX.

HOW SULTÁN 'ALÁ-UD-DÍN GOVERNED IN HIND.

When the counsellors assembled by his command had arrived at the conclusion that the numerous insurrections which had troubled the public weal had arisen from the Sultán's neglect of the business of the State, and addictedness to strong drinks, as also from the plethora of wealth which afflicted the Hindús of that period, and led to riots and revolts which they never would have thought of if they had had to live from hand to mouth, the Sultán came back from his hardly-won conquest of Ratambhor, and was wroth with the citizens of Dehlí. About this time his brother-scoundrel and assistant in the murder of his nonagenarian uncle, 'Ulugh Beg, died from the exposure and hardships of a campaign in the distant south, and the Sultán set seriously to work to prevent rebellion and to confiscate right and left.

Villages held in proprietary right, in free gift, or as religious endowments, were brought by a few strokes of the pen into the hands of the Exchequer.

Griping extortion plundered everyone who had means, and at length, with the exception of the horse-leeches of the Upper Ten Thousand of Hind, everyone became destitute of money. As capital had altogether disappeared, and folks were perforce compelled to toil for their day's bread, they had no leisure time to devote to sedition, and there were no "corner-groggery-rowdies" in the Dehlí of astute 'Alá-ud-dín, as there are and ever have been in the United States of America, for "whose idle hands, Satan," as good little Dr. Watts assures us, "finds some mischief still to do," notably in the time of a Presidential election in those Trans-Pontine regions.

Sharp and lynx-eyed were the spies, too, of this rigid monarch; into every home both of high and low, they penetrated, until no one dared to wag his tongue even within the precincts of his own dwelling, because sharp and sudden punishment surely followed the slightest accusation of the Sultán's *mouchards*. Not a dealer in the bázár could drive a bargain without the knowledge of this Paul Pry of a sovereign. Quitting the seducing goblet himself, and abandoning his former conviviality, he passed a sort of Maine Liquor or Lawsonian decree which forbade both the purchase and sale of intoxicating fluids. Gamblers were heavily visited. And yet all this severity failed to attain its end, for the obstinate still bought and sold clandestine wine and spirits, "shebeen-fashion," in every direction; sometimes the forbidden liquids were disguised in a leathern water-bag, at other times they were hidden in bundles of wood-faggots and in loads of hay. When seized, the wine and alcohol were made over to the royal elephants, who appear to have appreciated them highly, as did a very lively and, no doubt, very holy monkey, whom Il Musannif once possessed in the old post of Kángrá.

Dropping the offenders into deep pits outside the gates of Dehlí and half-starving them, proved of little avail, and unlimited bambooing failed to convert them. So when they began to find Dehlí too hot to hold them, as has happened in this nineteenth century in some other countries which are separated from the Continent of Europe by a mere strip of sea, the cauterization of the sore which had arisen from the evil humours of the blood, bone, and marrow, had its usual effect, although arresting the malady for awhile, of causing it to burst forth with increased virulence in another direction.

As the sons of Scotland walk from Edinburgh to

Leith or Dalkeith, as the inhabitants of London journey a short distance down the Thames on a Sunday morning to "refresh" themselves, as other parties have emigrated to quarters of our great metropolis, from those the former stainless reputation of which has now become a hissing and a reproach, so did the publicans, sinners, and drunkards of the city by the Jamna, seek pastures new some ten or twelve miles away, and there their ogies were held.

The "sheep of the prisons" were masters of the situation to such an extent that the people began to communicate by signs, and the Hindú race were so ground down by oppressive edicts and unsparing exactions, that if they had lived in a colder country they would have been too poverty-stricken to purchase the meanest clothing. As it was, a langútí sufficed for the majority; they were not allowed a horse, or even to chew their favourite pán or betel-nut.

Blows, imprisonment, and fetters, at the command of iron-handed and stony-hearted tax-gatherers, were the Sultán's gentle persuasives to the mild Hindú whose happy star had brought him beneath that beneficent ruler of Hind, Sultán 'Alá-ud-dín.

Woe to the aforesaid tax-gatherers if they betrayed their trust in the slightest degree, and, said the pious Kází Mughísu-d-dín of Bayánah, in reply to a question put to him by the Sultán, "To keep the Hindús in abasement is especially a religious duty, because they are the most inveterate enemies of the Prophet, who has commanded his followers to slay, plunder, and make them captive. 'Death or Islám' is the watchword of all true Musulmáns."

And when Il Musannif remembers the deadly mutiny of 1857, and sees the descendants of those same Muhammadans who caused it, whom we have ousted from their high places in that same land of Hind, and whose religious fanaticism and hatred of the Nazarene are but ill-concealed by that veneer of European civilisation which they have acquired in our own universities and schools, he looks forward with deep apprehension and anxiety to the day when the sword, which we have allowed men whom no benefits can render loyal to sharpen on our own grindstone, will decapitate that Empire of Hind of which we are now so proud.

XXXI.

DEHLÍ IN IMMINENT PERIL.

When Targhí "the Accursed" heard that Sultán 'Alá-ud-dín had gone to the siege of Chitor with every available man at arms, and that Dehlí was deprived of all its defenders, he made haste to come there with his Mughál hordes from far-away "Máwáru-n-Nahar"; and, at the same time, it chanced that the force which had for its object the reduction of Arangal in the south, had its onward progress arrested and its return hindered by the heavy tropical rains.

With an army sorely diminished in numbers before stubborn Chitor, did the Sultán hurry back towards his endangered capital, but was unable to enter its walls, inasmuch as more than 100,000 wild horsemen soon encompassed his diminished and dispirited troops, and blocked up the roads to the city.

From his leaguer at Sírí, where he entrenched himself so strongly that his adversaries did not venture to attack him, he beheld the invaders masters of the whole surrounding districts, which they pillaged and spoiled in Mughál fashion. Famine stared him in the face, and all seemed lost, when 'Alá-ud-dín was preserved by the sudden retreat of Targhí. In another month the fall of Dehlí would have been inevitable.

Awed by this narrow escape, the Sultán ceased to neglect home-cares, and turned from interference with his neighbours to fortifying himself in his central possessions, and by so augmenting his army as to render it in the future a thorough and efficient barrier against Mughál aggression.

Il Musannif knows well that it was a time-honoured custom of the Osmánlís of Istambúl to nail dishonest vendors of bread by the lobes of their ears with, no doubt, "a tenpenny (or it may be a five-ghrúsh) nail" to their own doors, but that was comparatively mild treatment to that which Sultán 'Alá-ud-dín meted out to his culprits.

To secure cheapness and fixed charges in the markets, the stick was very freely administered, *and flesh was cut from the haunches of those who gave short weight,* somewhat after the fashion of the treatment of oxen in Abyssinia in the days of Bruce, the traveller; a *very sore* regulation this, as cheats found it to be.

Better prepared now for the warm reception of his Mughál foes, he thoroughly repelled their next irruptions, and pyramids and towers of their skulls testified to the great defeat that had been inflicted on them, whilst their rotting carcases infected the surrounding atmosphere and were grateful to the nostrils of a victor who thought, with Charles IX. of France when he passed by the gibbeted corpse of the noble and murdered Admiral de Coligni at Montmartre, "that the smell of a dead enemy was always sweet."

XXXII.

HOW THE ARMY OF SULTÁN 'ALÁ-UD-DÍN GHILZAI MARCHED TO THE CONQUEST OF TÍLANG AND MALABÁR.

When the King had repelled the Mughál invasion under Kadur, whom the historian calls the Mú-Shikáf (or "Hair-Splitter"), on account of his intense subtlety, and those of other predatory hordes of the same nation, commanded by 'Alí Beg, Turtak, and other leaders, he overcame Gujarát, Somnát, Ratambhor, and Jhain, Málwa, Chitor, Deogír, and Síwána, and despatched his lieutenant Malik Káfúr towards the country of Tílang.

After traversing such a rough and inhospitable country, they looked on it as like unto Al-Sirat, or the "Razor-bridge of Hell," and fording many rivers, Khándhar was reached, and thence, through drenching rains, rocky and narrow ways, and raging torrents, to Sarbar, within the confines of Tílang. This place speedily fell into the hands of the followers of Islám, but Arangal was valiantly defended by the Hindús. The King's Deputy, therefore, ordered the *Western Stone-balls* (such as were discharged by the Osmánlís at Admiral Duckworth when he forced the passage of the Dardanelles, A.D. 1811) to be cast at the wall in order to pulverize it, and the catapults and balistas of the besiegers told with murderous effect on the beleaguered garrison.

Walls were raised which enabled the Sultán's soldiers to discharge their missiles downwards into the city, the defences of which were so well-battered that they no longer afforded good cover to their defenders; moreover, the shot of those *Western Engines*, the deadly cannons, had made many breaches, each destined to be "a Gate of Victory" to the royal troops.

On the night of the 11th of the month of holy Ramázán, in the year of "the Departure" 708, the stormers and scaling-ladders were held in readiness for the attack, which was covered by unceasing discharges of missiles of every description.

That night three of the outer bastions fell into the hands of the conquering Musulmáns, and on Sunday the 13th the assault was vigorously renewed amidst loud shouts of "Huzza huzz," and "Khuzza Khuzz," by the holy warriors of the faith, who thus proved conclusively that the "Huzza" or "Hurrah" of the west was of truly Oriental origin.

The outer circumvallation had been now captured, but the courageous Hindú Laddur Deo still held out for some time within his inner strong citadel. At last he offered terms of capitulation, which were, we may presume, only too acceptable to Malik Káfúr, considering his own difficult and precarious position in the midst of a hostile country and at so great a distance from any support; but we must leave to the grandiloquent scribe of this remarkable campaign to recount what subsequently occurred in his own inflated and exaggerated phraseology.

"When the messengers of Ráí Laddur Deo came before the canopy of red, which is the honoured harbinger of victory and triumph, they rubbed their yellow faces on the ground till the earth itself acquired their colour, and they drew out their tongues in elegant

Hindúí, more cutting than a Hindú sword [a sharp remark this of Mír Khusrú's], as they delivered the message of their Ráí.

"The 'Idol Breaker,' Malik Káfúr, received their gifts, and for the present suspended operations against the fort, but he demanded tribute of all that the Ráí possessed, down to vegetables, mines, and animals.

"On this condition the 'Fort-taking Malik,' [a sort of Oriental Demetrius Poliorcetes, no doubt, and who was a dissipated Eunuch into the bargain], returned his sword to its scabbard, and struck the backs of the messengers so forcibly with his open hand by way of admonition, that they bent under the blow. Tremblingly they hastened back to the fortress, where the Ráí passed the night in gathering together his wealth, and next morning his officers brought the elephants and spoil into the camp of the Muhammadans. Poll-tax, or jizza, was also to be sent punctually to the foot of the Imperial throne at Dehlí, and in March, 1310 A.D., the Malik departed from Arangal with all his booty, and no fewer than 1,000 camels groaned under the weight of the treasure which was presented to the sovereign on the 24th of Muharram, A.H. 710, in the Chautara Násira of the capital.

"Kings and princes of Arabia and Persia stationed themselves around, and famous chiefs who had fled to the city of Islám came to offer allegiance, and honoured the dust by prostrating their foreheads therein before the King. You would have said," continues the author of this narrative, "that the people looked on that day as a second Festival of 'Id, when the returning pilgrims, after passing safely through the trackless deserts, had arrived at the sacred threshold of the Sultán."

XXXIII.

MUHAMMAD BAKHTIYÁR GHILZAI IN BIHÁR AND BENGAL.

The bold and enterprising Muhammad Bakhtiyár was a Ghilzai, born in the hot land of Garmsír, and he sought service from Sultán Mu'izzu-d-dín of Ghazní; being dismissed from the office which he thus obtained, he directed his steps towards the rich Hindústán, as a hungry and ambitious Afghán almost invariably did. Under the auspices of Malik Hisámu-d-dín Ughlabak, he did such deeds of valour that the lands of Sahlat and Sahlí were conferred on him in jágír. From this point of vantage he made repeated incursions into the districts of Múnghír and Bihár, bringing back immense booty; and when the fame of his bravery and good fortune was noised abroad, a number of his own Ghilzai tribe joined his standard, and the Sultán Kutbu-d-dín bestowed on him robes of honour.

After surprising the fort of Bihár and putting all its

shaven and learned Brahmans to the edge of the sword, *more Musulmanico*, he presented himself and his spoil at the Court of Sultán Kutbu-d-dín, who showered so many bounties on him that the envy and jealousy of the courtiers vented themselves in jibes and irony.

Being dared to fight on foot with an elephant in the Court of the White Palace, he wounded it so sorely in the trunk with his battle-axe, that it turned and fled, after which not only did the Sultán gift him largely, but compelled the scorners to do the same.

Leaving Dehlí he returned to Bihár, and his name was the terror of the infidels of Lakhnautí, Bihár, Bengal, and Kámrúp.

Rái Lakhmaniyá at this time ruled in Nadiya, and strange was the story of his birth, which we give in the words of the chronicler, Minháju-s-Siráj.

"When the father of Rái left this world he was in the womb of his mother, so the crown was placed on her belly, and all the chiefs made obeisance before her; and when the time of her delivery grew near, she assembled the Brahmans and astrologers in order that they might ascertain whether the aspect of the time was auspicious. They all unanimously agreed that if the child were born at that moment it would be unlucky, and that he would never ascend the throne, but that if the birth occurred two hours later the child would reign for eighty years. When the mother heard this she ordered her legs to be tied together, and caused herself to be hung up with her head downwards, and when the auspicious moment arrived she was taken down and immediately gave birth to Lakhmaniya."

The devoted mother lost her life from the anguish she had endured (and no wonder! say we), but her son governed for the space of eighty years, and was the most just and generous sovereign of his time.

When his beneficent rule had continued some four-score years, he was warned by his astrologers that his possessions were doomed to become the prey of the Turks; and they foretold also that the invader and conqueror would be a man whose hands when he stood upright would hang to below his knees, so that he could touch his shins.

Such a phenomenon was found by the Ráí's envoys in the person of Muhammad Bakhtiyár, and the greater part of the Ráí's chiefs and Brahmans fled like cowards to the sacred country of Shank Nath or Jagannáth; but the aged Rájá would not stir from his place, and in the following year Muhammad Bakhtiyár came in peaceable and mercantile guise, and with only eighteen followers, to spy out the nakedness of the land.

Lulled by his wily and pacific demeanour, the unsuspecting Hindús made no preparation against his small following, thinking that he was a dealer in horses, and sorely disturbed was the Ráí's dinner-party when the handful of Afgháns suddenly rushed into the palace, and, after slaughtering many, plundered and sacked it, the octogenarian barely escaping barefooted in the confusion. Soon reinforced by the remainder of his troops, Muhammad Bakhtiyár took possession of his easy conquest and fixed his head-quarters there.

Truly, in that effeminate land of Lower Bengal, the old Spanish saying concerning Andalusia held good then as it does to this day, "that the earth is water, and that the men are women."

Ráí Lakhmaniya, or Lakshmana, found shelter in Orissa, where he died, and where his descendants governed in after years.

Dissatisfied with Nadiya, Muhammad Bakhtiyár razed it to the ground, and made Lakhnautí the seat of his Government, and this great city was also known as Gaur.

Situated on low eminences in the district of Maldah, and on the banks of that Bhágírathí, which was once the main channel of the Ganges, its vast ruins still excite the wonder of the traveller. Major Rennell says that its extent, at the most reasonable calculation, is not less than fifteen miles in length, and from two to three in breadth; several villages stand on part of its site, and the remaining space is either a wild jungle, the home of the prowling tiger and of other *feræ naturæ*, or cultivated fields whose soil is of brickdust.

Once in secure possession of Gaur, Muhammad Bakhtiyár, although he paid nominal fealty to his ancient sovereign, Sultán Kutbu-d-dín, and shared his plunder with him, asserted his independence practically by causing the Khutba to be read in his own name and imprinted on the coinage, as is the wont of all Muhammadan sovereigns at the period of their accession to regal authority.

Well did the stalwart and cunning Afghán know that the hand of the King of Dehlí was too feeble to assail him in the far-off swamps and delta of Lower Bengal.

XXXIV.

A MUSSULMÁN INVASION OF TIBET.

Guided by 'Alí Mích, a converted Hindú from the hills which divide the territory of Lakhnautí from the uplands of Tibet, Muhammad Bakhtiyár came to the city Maidán-Kot, by which ran the great river Brahmaputra, which at its estuary, in the Gulf of Bengal, was known to the Hindús by the name of "Samundar," or "the Sea." For two weary days did the army of the Muhammadans toil along the banks of the mighty stream, through the mountains, till they came to an ancient bridge of twenty arches of stone.

There Muhammad Bakhtiyár posted a strong force

to hinder his return from being intercepted, and then went dashingly forward into what was to him an unknown land, little heeding the warnings of the then friendly Rájá of Kámrúp, who told him that with such insufficient means he would run great risk of disaster and disgrace.

But frequent previous successes had blinded the Afghán chief to the perils of this new enterprise, and he paused not in the execution of his purpose.

Halting one night in the year of "the Departure" of the Prophet from Mecca 641, between Deokot and Bangáwan, he learned from an old comrade that his onward road lay for fifteen stages through defiles and passes, and that on reaching the fifteenth stage his eyes would be gladdened by the sight of a well-peopled and fertile country.

The natives stood their ground sturdily as he advanced, and at the very first village numbers of his soldiers were slain or wounded by the enemy, who plied their bamboo-spears and jávelins with deadly dexterity. After passing this place the warriors of Islám became dismayed when they heard that in their front lay the strong city of Karambatan, defended by many valiant Buddhists, armed with bows. Wise when it was too late, Muhammad Bakhtiyár resolved on retreat, and as he retired he found that the hill-men had so desolated the country that not a blade of grass nor a twig of wood were obtainable. All the inhabitants had fled into the jungles, and as no grain or forage could be procured during fifteen days of despair, the horses were sacrificed to alleviate the cravings of hunger. Backward trudged the famished and foot-sore invaders until they reached the bridge before mentioned, only to find that, taking advantage of a quarrel between the two officers left in charge of it, the Hindús, who knew what to expect from the tender mercies of their Islámite foes, had broken down the arches and removed or destroyed all the boats.

Posting himself in a strong idol-temple, the chieftain looked around him to discover some means of crossing the broad and deep river; but here the hitherto apparently amicable Rájá of Kámrúp raised the country and so beleaguered him in his stronghold that he and his soldiers, fearful of being starved to death, or of partaking the same fate which they had so often and so unsparingly meted out to others, charged desperately out and cut their way to the river's bank.

Closely pursued by the Hindús, most of Muhammad Bakhtiyár's men-at-arms met with a watery grave whilst striving to swim their horses to the opposite bank, and the crest-fallen chief of Lakhnautí, with but 100 others, were the sole survivors of this rash expedition.

Compelled to halt at Deokot through the sickness of disappointment and grief, he became a butt for the abuse of the wives and families of those who had perished, and who had all that volubility of vituperation of which indignant females of both east and west are well-known to have so ready a command.

From every house-top maledictions hailed on him, until he shrank from the public gaze and took to his bed and died, not without suspicion of assassination, for another Afghán of the same treacherous race as himself, 'Alí Maidán Ghilzai, is asserted to have found means to enter his private apartment and to deal him a death-blow with a dagger, in the year of "the Departure" 602, corresponding to A.D. 1205.

The murderer escaped, and so ingratiated himself with the Sultán Kutbu-d-dín that he gave him the government of Lakhnautí; but his tyranny brought him to an evil end; certain of the Ghilzai chiefs, who had suffered many wrongs at his hands, conspired and put him to death.

Ought not the History of Hind to be penned in letters of blood?

XXXV.

KUTBU-D-DÍN'S SECOND VISIT TO AJMÍR.

When—to use the strong expressions generally employed by Musulmán annalists when referring to "the black-faced and infidel Hindús"—Kutbu-d-dín had sent the infidels who were so blinded as to adhere to the faith of their forefathers, and who dwelt in the country of Kol, "to the fire of Hell, by the edge of the sword," and had cemented together so many of their skulls as to form three high bastions, whilst their carcases were abandoned to those hosts of vultures, crows, kites, wolves, and jackals who followed the destroying track of every Muhammadan horde through devastated Hind, with unerring prescience of a rich repast, he returned to Dehlí, and administered justice with such impartiality "that wolves and sheep drank water out of the same pool."

Disturbed, however, from his dreams of beneficence by the tidings that the Ráí of Ajmír, Hiráj, "had raised the standards of perdition and opened the road of rebellion," and that Jihtar, that other dark-minded unbeliever, had aided and abetted him by an incursion into the borders of Dehlí, and retaliated in sanguinary fashion on the Muhammadan populations, Kutbu-d-dín set forth towards Ajmír in the middle of the hot season, "when the armour on the bodies of the valiant was inflamed by the heat of the sun, and the sword in the scabbard melted like wax, so that he was compelled to march by night, just as Il Musannif has had to do when on treasure-escort.

Flying before the resolute Muhammadan chief, Jihtar sought refuge in the strong fortress of Ajmír, where he immolated himself and his wives and children by fire.

The usual massacres and destruction of idols, with their inseparable accompaniments of unsparing plunder and rapine, followed in due course, and then, "the road of rebellion being closed, the religion of Islám being re-established, infidelity being exterminated, and oppressed True Believers relieved from their oppressors," the victorious Kutbu-d-dín returned in state to the capital.

Another of the many instances in which the spasmodic but not all-enduring bravery of the Rajpúts failed to recover their independence, and only strengthened the hands of their tyrants.

XXXVI.

HOW KANAUJ FELL BEFORE MAS'ÚD THE THIRD, AND HOW THE SCRIBE ALÁ-UD-DAULA MAS'ÚD BEWAILED HIS CAPTIVITY.

"When the chief of the Faithful, by the aid of the Prophet, collected a vast army and turned, as a holy warrior [or Ghází], towards the land of Hind, with many brave Turks in his company, they placed chains on the feet and a collar on the neck of Mulhí, the God-forgotten chief of Hind, and bore him before the king. Kanauj was the Pole-star of Hindú heathens, and all the riches and wealth of the country were concentrated within it. Black was his countenance, demoniacal his actions, and his religion was sorcery, whilst his disposition was that of a tiger whom the foul Fiend had begotten. From the rain of swords which the men of Sultán Mahmúd showered on his unbelievers, the very earth of Hindústán was reddened, and that creature of the family of Hell fled from the wrath of the sons of Islám."

After this laudation of his Sovereign, poor Sa'd Salmán, in the nineteenth year of his captivity, moans most piteously, "My body is as attenuated as a hair, my heart is on fire, and I tear my chest *with my long blue nails* in my anguish. Fifty years of good service have been of no account, for my foes hold my well-won estates, and I am still a miserable prisoner in a hill-fortress [or Oriental Bastille], and in the nineteenth year of the vilest durance; yet I never turned my back on my Lord the Sultán's foe, for I and mine have been his slaves during seven generations."

When the poet died about the year of the Christian Era, 1131, he *may* have been once more a free and happy man, but inasmuch as it is still the base practice of interested subordinates in all lands to "burke" the complaints of those who have suffered grievous wrong at their hands, and to prevent them from reaching the ears of well-meaning superiors, it is extremely probable that Khwájah Salmán languished in his obscure dungeon until life departed, much as the prisoners of the inglorious Bourbons did in the Bastille of Saint Antoine, until the "*Red Caps*" *capsized* them.

XXXVII.

THE PRINCE OF MARTYRS.

When the Rájás of the Hindús made ready to resist the forces of Mas'úd the Ghaznawíde, they mustered their forces, and foremost amongst them stood Sahar Deo from Shabhún, and courageous Nar Deo of Balúna; then the blacksmiths were made to prepare 5,000 metal balls, each armed with five poisoned prongs, and to fix them firmly in the earth before the commencement of the battle. "When the Musulmáns charge," said these chiefs, "the prongs will pierce the feet of their chargers, and when they are down we will stab and hack them in revenge for the many wrongs we have endured at their hands."

Then the allied Hindú Rái warned Prince Mas'úd to depart from the country of their forefathers if he loved his own life, but he boldly answered them in this wise. "Through the grace of God, my steps have not yet turned back, and by His assistance they shall not do so now; the country is God's, and the property of him on whom He bestows it. Who gave it to your fathers and ancestors?"

Then the Martyr-Prince buckled on his armour and rode to the encounter of the unbelievers; but the stratagems of the wary Hindús, who also made plentiful use of rockets, lamed the steeds of the Faithful, and terrified them beyond control, so that one-third of

Mas'úd's warriors fell to rise no more in this fierce and indecisive combat, and, in the phraseology of the devout author, "tasted the wine of martyrdom."

The youth Mas'úd, for he was but nineteen years of age, now found a short respite from the toils of war in the spacious and beautiful gardens with which he had adorned Bahráích, until the Hindús gathered once more against him, "like swarms of ants or locusts," and beleaguered his camp.

On the 18th day of the month Rajabu-l-Murajjab in the year 424, at break of day, the unbelievers attacked the van of the army, and great and indecisive was the carnage which ensued.

But the heathen were too numerous for the far smaller army of the Muhammadans, who fought with all the exaltation of fanaticism, until one of their best leaders, Sálá Saifu-d-dín, was numbered with the slain, thus sealing his faith with his blood, and scarcely a handful of fighting men remained alive around Prince Mus'úd.

First looking to the interment of his dead comrades, and rejoicing in the immediate prospect of becoming a martyr for the faith, he boldly met the onset of the Hindú reserves, commanded by Ráís Sáhár Deo and Har Deo, who threw themselves in masses against his enfeebled and scanty squadrons.

Driven back to the shelter of that very garden which he had himself planted, and which had been to him a place of dalliance and a pleasaunce in more peaceful days, he stood there at bay, never quailing before the shafts which the beleaguering Hindús poured remorselessly upon him and his little band of heroes, until on the 14th day of June, A.D. 1033, just thirty-three years before our own battle of Hastings, as the time of evening-prayer approached, an arrow pierced the main artery of the arm of this "Prince of the Faithful." His sunlike countenance became of the pallor of the new moon, and, with the text in praise of martyrdom on his lips, he dismounted from his horse. With his head on the lap of his faithful follower Sikandar Díwání, he gazed in the direction of Mecca, and tears dropped from his eyes. So the "Prince of Martyrs" rendered up his soul to his Maker, and noble Sikandar still remained supporting the head of his dead master, and died in that posture.

And the idolators banished the creed of Islám entirely from the land, and re-established their idols for the space of two hundred years.

XXXVIII.

SULTÁN SHAMSU-D-DÚNIYÁ WA UD-DÍN ABÚ-L-MUZAFFAR ALTAMSH.

AND a very pretty little title he assumed, did this Indian commander of those "faithful" men who believed that it was his and their special mission to act after the fashion of Joshua, the son of Nun, and to waste and plunder all the countries of those of other creeds, and *sharply* convert them to the "Dínu-s-Saif," or "Sabre-Religion," after smashing their graven images and relieving them of all their sub-lunary belongings, the last being regarded as the most important tenet inculcated by Him of Mecca on all True Believers.

Now, being interpreted, the name of Altamsh (which was his original Tátár cognomen) has added to it, in grandiloquent style, as written at the heading of this episode, "The Monarch, Sun of both Earth and Religion, the Father of the Conqueror."

Witness the learned Kází, Minháju-s-Siráj, who was regarded as "the wonder of his time and the most eloquent man in Persia," who was Court-preacher to Sultán Altamsh, and who thus speaks of his Imperial patron.

"It is related by persons worthy of belief, that this monarch was selected by Providence from the tribe of Albarí, in Turkistán, to rule for Islám over the realm of Hind. His father, Yalam Khán, was well to do and powerful, and his beauty and intelligence created such jealousy in the hearts of his brothers, that they enticed him away from his parents under the pretext of showing him some fine horses. His case was as that of Joseph. They said to his father, 'Why do you not trust him with us, that he may disport himself in our company, whilst we look after him with fraternal affection?' "

But when they came with their brother to the horse-dealer, they treated him as the brethren of Joseph had treated him, and sold him as a slave to the merchant of equine quadrupeds.

Luck, however, did not desert him, and he was adopted into the family of the wealthy and influential Chief Judge of Bukhárá, who chanced to become his next purchaser.

Being once sent by some member of his master's family to buy grapes in the bázár, the boy lost his money, or it was filched from him by some Bukhárian ancestor of Charles Dickens's "Noah Claypole," who was on the "Kinchin lay"; and while he was bewailing his loss, in fear of chastisement, a good old fakír took compassion on him, and after purchasing the required fruit with some copper coins from his own girdle, which, after the manner of the East, served him in lieu of a pocket, told him, that when he attained wealth and power he should always bear in mind that it was his bounden duty and nearest interest to care for and protect the pious poor.

Then he passed from hand to hand, as human cattle did in those fine old days of Islám, until he fell under the eyes of Sultán Mu'izzu-d-dín Muhammad Sám at Ghazní, where his price became a bone of contention between his owner, the slave-merchant Jamálu-d-dín

Chast Kabá, and the Sultán. Finally, he was sold to Kutbu-d-dín, and was placed at the head of the guards in Dehlí. He now rose rapidly, and was made Chief Huntsman and Amír of Gwáliár after the conquest of that fortress.

Mightily did he distinguish himself against the Gakkars on the banks of the Jhailaur, and his deeds of valour on that occasion made him a free man.

Named after the decease of Kutbu-d-dín to the sovereignty of Dehlí, he utterly beat and discomfited all those who stood in his path, and firmly established his authority.

In the year of the Hijrah 622, he carried his arms to the distant land of Gaur; in the succeeding year the strong fortress of Ratambhor succumbed to him, and after he had won Mandúr, in the hills of Síwalik, and other citadels, he made himself master of Uch.

Even to the capital of Islám, at Baghdád, did the renown of this zealous warrior of Islám extend, and great were the gifts and magnificent were the dresses sent to Shamsu-d-dín by the successor of the Prophet.

After slaughtering the rebellious of Gwáliár in wholesale fashion, "this pure, generous, heroic, and *kindly* king" turned his attention to the unfortunate Hindús of Málwa, Bhílsa, and Ujjain, in which latter city he smote down and demolished the image of the renowned Vikramáditya and the temple of Mahá-Kálí, together with herself, her Briarean and weaponed-hands, and her inhuman necklace of human skulls.

Forced, finally, by severe sickness to withdraw from an expedition against Multán, he barely lived to reach Dehlí, where he died in the month of April, A.D. 1235, after having reigned not less than six-and-twenty years.

XXXIX.

AMÍR KHUSRÚ THE POET.

THIS worthy, whose name has been elsewhere mentioned by Il Musannif, was in the service of Khán Jahán, with whom he remained for the space of two years in the province of Oudh (or Awadh), whilst his old mother was in Dehlí, telling over the beads of her rosary, and sorrowing for his return, as mothers will do even in Eastern lands. One day he took some of her letters to his master, who munificently gifted him with two trays filled with gold to defray the expenses of his journey.

"I had travelled one whole month," says the poet, "*without drawing rein* [Il Musannif allows a good deal for Oriental exaggeration], when I at last reached Dehlí in the month of Zí-l-Káda, and was restored to life after death. I placed my head at the feet of my mother, who embraced me, with tears in her eyes, and after a brief space I was summoned into the presence of the Sultán by one of his Chamberlains."

Ready armed with a laudatory poem, which he duly recited, he received a dress of honour, two bags of money, and was enrolled amongst the personal attendants of the King. Moreover, as he proudly relates with poetic pride, the Sultán called him "the most perfect of poets, whose very crumbs other poets were glad to pick up." After displaying a vast amount of mock modesty, he was requested to write an account in verse of an interview between the present Sultán and his honoured and deceased father.

Secluding himself for this laudable purpose from all society for six months, in order to arrive as near perfection as possible, he completed his task within the given time, and it must have been a rather long-winded piece of business, seeing that the poem consisted of 3,944 verses. Pleasing as such adulation in superior Persian rhyme may have been to the object of his flattery, Il Musannif would rather not inflict such a dose on his readers, and he, therefore, confines himself to the following extract, much trimmed of its original verbiage:—

"Each [father and son] is asked by the other to accept the crown, when the younger said to the elder that the throne was his of right, and that he was his willing slave. The father insisted on his son taking precedence of him."

But after much such gentle altercation, the father led his son by the hand up the steps of the throne, and then stood humbly before him. Then, as the father departed across the river, his son festively filled his own boat with wine "and all immersed themselves in the vinous bath till they were drunk, and lost their respect for the King, together with their own senses."

Next day the monarchy was formally conferred on the son, and after an affectionate parting, each took his own way, and the younger man drowned his sorrow in the flowing bowl ; a much pleasanter termination to a family discord than was the general rule in Oriental lands.

XL.

THE BEAUTEOUS DEWÁL DEVÍ.

A SOMEWHAT romantic interest attaches to the story of this bright Hindú maiden, not only because of her adventures, but because her case shows how the most bigoted Rájpút chiefs often yielded up their daughters even to the hated Musulmán, violating their own religion thereby.

The wife of the Rájá of Gujrát had been taken by the invaders in former years, and became the highly-favoured spouse of the Sultán 'Alá-ud-dín, and when she heard that Alp Khán's road to the siege of Deogírí lay through Bázlána, where her former lord had taken refuge, she besought the Emperor to cause his general to recover her lost daughter by her first marriage, the lovely Dewál Deví.

The overtures made by Alp Khán in consequence were unhesitatingly rejected by the Rájpút Rájá, who had already refused her hand to the low-caste, albeit powerful, Maratha chief of Deogírí. Notwithstanding his previous objections, however, his hatred of Islám led him to prefer even a Maratha to a Muhammadan, and the poor princess was sent in haste to wed the Chief of Deogírí.

Incensed at the slight thus put upon him, and terrified lest his non-fulfilment of the mandate of his Imperial master should subject him to the direst of penalties, Alp Khán directed his arms against the recalcitrant father, whom he put utterly to the rout and pursued through the mountains for several days, until his track was lost, and no tidings could be procured of the whereabouts either of the Rájá or of his fair daughter.

Now it so happened that a party of his horsemen encountered and defeated a body of Maratha horse, commanded by the brother of the Rájá of Deogírí, who were conveying the maiden to that place. The girl's horse was pierced by an arrow, and the victors contended so savagely with each other for the possession of so charming a spoil that she would have been slain in the scuffle had not one of her attendants implored them to spare the unhappy Dewál Deví.

No sooner was her name and quality known than they shrunk away in terror of the consequences of their maltreatment of the daughter of their Queen, and she was borne with high honour and respect to Dehlí and restored to her mother.

There she soon enthralled the affections of the King's eldest son, Khizr Khán, to whom she was given in marriage; and is not the history of their loves written in noble verse by the famed poet, Amír Khusrú?

XLI.

THE "'ASHIKA" (OR "LOVED ONE") OF AMÍR KHUSRU.

We must now complete our former episode of the adventures of that Dewál Rání whom we left the happy bride of Prince Khizr, the eldest son of the Sultán 'Alá-ud-dín.

At first suspected and confined by his own parent, after the death of the latter, the traitor, would-be usurper, and eunuch-parasite Malik Náib Káfúr deprived the unfortunate Prince of his eye-sight; and when Kutbu-d-dín Mabárak Sháh came to the throne, he, in compliance with that ferocious Oriental policy which invariably sends to the shambles every possible claimant to the seat of royalty, delivered the sightless Khizr and all his brethren into the hands of the executioner, a functionary who was ever active in those sanguinary old times of "the Romantic Land of Hind."

The fate of the luckless Rájpút princess is wrapped in mystery. Poet Khusrú affirms that she lost her hands by the sword whilst they enclasped the body of her husband; whilst old Farishta says that she was forced into first the harem of King Kutbu-d-dín, and then into the seraglio of the ruffian Khusrú Khán, whom we must by no means confound with her eulogist the gentle poet Khusrú.

In this poem, which he wrote in Khizr's better days and at his request, he thus praises his native country of happy Hindústán—"Where," says he, "the vapours of infidelity have been dispersed by the swords of our holy warriors, where the strong Hindú infidels must perforce pay tribute, where Islám is triumphant, and idolatry overcome.

"Not a Christian *who does not fear to render the servant equal to God*, not a Jew who dares to raise the Pentateuch to a level with the Kurán, and not one of those Magi who delighted in their Fire Worship.

"The very fish are Sunnís," says the exulting Khusrú, "and all four sects of the Musulmáns are bound by the tie of brotherhood."

XLII.

AMÍR KHUSRÚ ON THE LANGUAGES OF HIND.

THE great poet above named, and whom Il Musannif but lately left a captive in the unclean hands of Mughal freebooters, thus speaks in his *brief* dissertation on the tongues of India. As it is not as *lengthy and grievously tedious* as many more modern and European treaties on the same subject, Il Musannif makes no scruple in quoting it "verbatim."

"It is well known that the languages of conquering races have by degrees mingled themselves with the original speech, and become the common language of the country; as had been the case in Baghdád, where originally but little Persian was spoken, and where, when the Khiláfat fell and the people of Párs dominated the Arab race, the *Arab herd* learned to respect the language of their *shepherds*. The city, which was originally *Baghdád* in Arabic, was Persianized into *Bághchah-dád*."

Turkí became just as prevalent when the Turks mastered the land, and "the language of the chiefs bore fruit on a new soil" ("A very nice metaphor, O Amír Khusrú!" says Il Musannif).

"Hind has observed the same rule; its language of old was Hindúí. When the tribes, great and small, became intermixed, everyone learnt Persian, and all the other languages remained unchanged. With the exception of Arabic, which, in consequence of the Kurán being written in it, is the most excellent and eloquent of languages, all tongues differ from one another, and each has some peculiar merit of its own. This one exclaims, 'My wine is better than that of others,' '*Everyone loses himself in his own cup, and no one admits that his own wine is vinegar.*'

"As I, Amír Khusrú, was born in Hind, I may be allowed to say a word respecting its languages. There is at this time (*i.e.* in the earlier portion of the fourteenth century, A.D.) in every province a language peculiar to itself, and not borrowed from any other, Sindhí, Lahâwarí, Kashmírí, Dhúr Samandar, Tilang, Gujarát, Mábár, Gaur, Bengal, Awádh, Dehlí, and its environs.

"But there is another language more select than the others, which all the Brahmans use. Its name from of old is 'Sahaskrit,' [*sic.*], and the common folk are unacquainted with it; whilst the male Brahman has it at his fingers' ends, his own wife knows nothing about it. It bears a resemblance to Arabic in some respects, in its permutations of letters, its grammar, its conjugations, and its polish.

"They have four books in that language, which they are constantly in the habit of repeating, and which are known under the name of 'Bed.' They contain stories of their gods, but little advantage can be derived from their perusal. Whatever other stories and fables they have are contained in 'kabits,' '*pauwánas*,' and 'námahs.'

"Their language possesses rules for composition and eloquence. The language is very precious, inferior to Arabic, but superior to Darí, and though the latter is certainly sweet and melodious, yet, even in that respect, this language does not yield to it."

XLIII.

'UNSURÍ THE POET.

Now, amongst the many poets who were received and entertained at the Court of the great Sultán Mahmúd of Ghazní, none rose to such eminence as Abú-l-Kásim Hasan bin Ahmad 'Unsurí, who came from the land of Balkh; and here is one of the laudatory odes that this Asiatic forerunner of the recluse of the Isle of Wight addressed to his patron:—

"Oh! thou who hast in history read of the merits of Kings, come hither and clearly view the grandeur of the Khusrú of Irán. His face will be found to be more beneficial than the sun itself, and his wealth is more abundant than the sand of the desert or the drops of a shower. Heroic in every deed, he is an eager lion-hunter; his army is as inseparable as a ring; when he rides he is a very Centaur, and the dust which is caused by his horse's hoofs obscures the sun; his steed's neigh deafens the heavens. With head erect and vengeful soul, he rushes on his prey as does the maned lion in his fury. Root and branch have his foes been exterminated, as were the tribes of 'Ad.

"When the troops of the Hindú Jaipál, which outnumbered the stars of the firmament, encountered him, his soldiers so imbued their swords in the blood of the infidels that they were as red as the morning-dawn. The Lord of Khurásán dispersed those Hindús on the plain of Peshâwar. How he overcame Multán has been eloquently related by Abu-l-Fazl Baihakí; and when he crossed the Chináb, the Indus, the Rávi, and the Jelam, he had neither boat nor anchor. On his road to Multán he captured 200 forts, each of which exceeded in strength the strong Khaibar of Arabia. Sneering at his adversaries and trampling on their bodies, he rooted out the glorious gardens of Gang and Tháneswar, because they were idol-shrines and places of pilgrimage for the benighted Hindús. Down went the broken-up idol of Somnát at the entrance of the Great Mosque of Ghazní; still will the blood of his enemies continue to flood the plains of Hind.

"Who, except God the Giver, can tell what booty this Prince brought back in grand procession? The desert-dust does not exceed the heaps of jewels which were piled up before the King of the World."

So far with our poet-laureate of Ghazní; but how sad must have been the day when the dying ravager of other lands, who felt that the hand of death was on him, caused all his spoils to be exhibited before him, and wept bitterly when he saw that his career was near its close, and that his possessions would fall into the hands of others. Well said old Shaikh Sa'dí of Shíráz in the second "Hikáyat" of the First Book of his "Rose Garden":—

"One of the monarchs of Khurásán saw Sultán Mahmúd Sabuktagín in a dream a hundred years after his death, when the whole of his carcase had been scattered and had become dust, excepting his eyes, which still revolved within their sockets as of yore, and looked around. All the wise were unable to explain this dream, except a darwesh, who came forward and said, 'His eyes are still glancing at his possessions which have fallen to others.'"

XLIV.

THE TIGER KING.

WHEN the outspoken Afghán, Shír Khán, came to pay homage to the great Mughal Emperor Bábar, there were two tigers in Agrá; for the name of each had a "tigerish" signification.

Victor over his adversaries in his own province of Bihár, he keenly watched the Mughal adversaries of his race who were then the masters of the land, hoping some day to revive that ancient supremacy which the Afgháns had lost through their own feuds and internal dissensions.

"Since I am among the Mughals," said he, "and know their conduct in action, I see that they have no order or discipline, and that their kings, from pride of birth or station, do not personally superintend the government, but leave the affairs of State to their nobles and ministers, in whose words and deeds they have perfect faith, although these evil and corrupt persons afflict and oppress their subjects, be they soldiers, cultivators, or zamíndárs. Whoever has money, whether loyal or disloyal, can get his business settled as he desires by means of bribery; but the man who carries no money in his girdle, although he may have proved his faith and loyalty on a hundred occasions, or may be a scarred veteran of many fights, he will never gain his end."

Rough soldier as he was, the Bihár Tiger could affect no refinement even in the presence and when the guest of the genial and courteous Bábar. Once at an entertainment he cut up a solid piece of meat with his dagger, much as he would have done in a bivouac, and devoured it after the fashion of the animal whose name he bore, and to the deep disgust of the courtly Mughals.

But the keen Emperor soon discerned that beneath this rough and uncouth exterior were concealed great talents, high courage, and lofty and ambitious aspirations, and he said to his minister Khalífah, who was standing at his side, "Keep an eye on Shír Khán, he is an able man, and the signs of royalty are visible on his forehead. I have seen many Afghán nobles of far higher station than he, but they failed to impress me as he has done. As soon as I beheld this man I thought to have him arrested, for he will, sooner or later, prove a fire-brand in the State."

True words, O Bábar, as the fate of thy son and successor, Humáyún, too surely proved in after days.

But the sharp Afghán chief had not failed to notice the conversation between the Sultán and his minister, and he intuitively felt that he had been the subject of it, so when he reached his own quarters on that day he thus spoke to his men: "The Emperor to-day looked much at me, said something to the minister, and cast evil glances at me. It is not good that I should remain," so he mounted his steed without delay, and fled from the camp.

Then he went back to his own jágír, and Sultán Muhammad Khán received him in amicable fashion, and bestowed the guardianship of his own son Jalál Khán on him. But when Sultán Muhammad died his concubine Dúdú constituted herself Regent of Bihár and its dependencies, and appointed Shír Khán her deputy; then the King of Gaur and Bengal conceived the design of conquering Bihár from its Afghán possessors, and he especially bore enmity towards Makhdúm Khán, the ruler of Hájípúr and the intimate ally of Shír Khán. So on came his general Kutb Khán with a powerful body of troops; then said Shír Khán to his Afghans, "With the Mughals on one side and the army of Bengal on the other, we must depend on our own valour alone for safety," and the Afgháns replied that he might be of good cheer, as they would win the field or die rather than prove ungrateful to the chief they had served so long.

So Shír Khán met the enemy, and, after a fierce battle, put them utterly to the rout, and slew Kutb Khán their leader. Much treasure, horses, and elephants, and other booty fell into the hands of Shír Khán, and the hitherto needy Afghán chief was now a man of wealth and substance.

But as he had kept all the spoil to himself and bestowed not a tittle on the Loháni Afgháns, the warriors of that tribe were exceedingly wroth.

When a second army advanced from Bengal against Makhdúm 'Alam, the enmity of the Lohánís prevented Shír Khán from succouring his friend, who fell in battle, after having made Shír Khán the heir of all his worldly possessions.

The Lohánís conspired the assassination of Shír Khán, but failed, because their machinations were known to him, and he made constant additions to the number of his retainers, whose hearts he rejoiced by his generosity.

At last, when he felt himself strong enough to contend with his foes, he spoke in this wise to the youthful King Jalál Khán, "You know that the Lohánís are a much more powerful tribe than those of Súr, *and the custom of the Afgháns is, that, if any man has four kinsmen more than another, he thinks little of killing or dishonouring his neighbour.* I know that the Lohánís are plotting my death, so in the future I shall only come to the palace with a strong guard of armed men."

A fresh war with the King of Bengal broke out, and, with a handful of his Afgháns, the superior generalship and courage of "the Tiger" proved too much for the effeminate troops whom Ibráhím Khán had led from the province of Lower Bengal.

To quote the words of the annalist 'Abbás Khán, "the sun of victory arose in favour of Shír Khán from the horizon of the East," and Ibráhím was amongst the slain.

One of Shír Khán's practices about this time was to wander at night about the bázárs of Bihár, and when he passed by any poor destitute man who was sleeping, after the fashion of the natives of India, on the bare ground and in the open air, to place gold and raiment beneath his pillow. Once a darwesh, who on awaking had found himself so suddenly enriched by an unknown hand, raised his head and cried, "Praise be to God, the Sultán of Dehlí has come!"

These words fell like music on the ears of the ambitious and superstitious Khán, who believed them to be divinely inspired, and never faltered in his endeavours to fulfil the utterances of the mendicant.

Now the Emperor Humáyún put his army in battle-array, and came to Kanauj to meet Shír Sháh in the month of Zí-l-Ka'da, A.H. 946, and the sturdy Afghán defied the Mughals to encounter him across the Ganges.

Although recommended by his chiefs to attack the Imperial army during the passage of the river, Shír the Chivalrous flatly refused to do so, saying, "I have never before had any advantages, and have been compelled to use stratagems in warfare. Now, by the favour of the All-Powerful, my force is not inferior to that of the Emperor. I will not, since I invited him across, and he has accepted my challenge, break faith in the face of day, but will give battle in the open field."

Entrenching himself, as was his custom, behind light earth-works, he made ready for the approaching action, and stimulated his men to daring deeds by stirring words and promises of great rewards.

After a roughly-contested battle, in which the final result seemed most uncertain for a time, and in which both monarchs displayed great bravery, Humáyún fled in hot haste towards Agra, whilst a great portion of his troops perished in the Ganges, "that blood-thirsty whirlpool," as the chroniclers of this event call it.

From Agra the Emperor, overpowered by the superstitious belief that his defeat had been owing to the intervention of supernatural agency, turned the heads of his horses in the direction of Lahore. As Shír Sháh advanced, his detachments spread themselves right and left throughout all districts, overcoming all those who still remained loyal to the discomfited son of Bábar, whose subsequent mischances will be related hereafter.

Then, being master of the greater part of Upper Hind, he betook himself to extend his conquests.

Say what his adversaries may, the brave "Tiger" was no usurper; a Hindústání by birth, he had expelled a race of outsiders whose rule was but fourteen years old.

Then he founded the great fortalice of Rhútás in the Upper Panjáb, calling it after its namesake of Bihár.

In the course of another year Málwa fell into his hands, and with no small degree of subterfuge and treachery were the Hindú defenders of the hitherto unconquered stronghold of Ráisín cut to pieces.

In the year 1544 of the Christian Era he fought with Rájá Máldeo of Márwár; and when every recourse to wile and foul play had failed to win success, the brave and desperate Rájpút was with difficulty repelled from his fierce attack on the Afghán camp.

But the end of the man who had retrieved the warlike reputation of those of Afghán blood who lived in Hindústán, and had become passingly effeminate amidst the hot winds of Upper and Central India, and the swamps and fevers of Lower Bengal, was near at hand.

After he had brought the Ráná of Mewár to his footstool as a humble suppliant for clemency, he laid siege to Barsingh Deo, Bundela, who had taken refuge in the citadel of Kalinjar with its Rájá, Kirát Singh.

So the fort was invested until the mounds raised against it overtopped its battlements, and the Afgháns of the King easily shot down the defenders in the very streets.

But the monarch hesitated to carry the besieged city by assault, fearing much that the general license which prevails on such occasions would cause risk to the safety of one whom he loved well if not wisely.

Within those walls was pent a maid (?), who was a Pátar slave-dancing-girl of the Kalinjar Rájá, Kirát Singh; the "jauhar" of the Hindús, in which a reckless sacrifice of all the defenders, and of their women and children would inevitably occur, was to be thought of, and so the assault was delayed.

As many versions of the death of Shír Sháh have

found their way into print, we prefer to select the account of his historian 'Abbás Khán, who wrote by order of the sublime and generous Akbar, who respected a valiant enemy with all the chivalry of his nature.

"On Friday, the 9th of Rabíu-l-awwal, 952 A.H., when one watch [pahr] and two hours of the day were over, Shír Sháh demanded his breakfast, which he ate in company with his men of learning and his priests, without whom he never took food. In the course of the meal Shaikh Nízám remarked, 'There is nothing equal to a religious war against the infidels. If you are slain you become a martyr, if you live you become a ghází.'

"When they had finished their repast, he ordered Dariyá Khán to bring loaded shells (or rockets, for the meaning in the text is uncertain), and pending their arrival he shot many arrows at the enemy from his own bow. When Dariyá Khán came forward, rather tardily, with the required missiles, they were so clumsily discharged that one which had stricken the gate of the fort recoiled amongst the others and caused their explosion.

"Right and left went the iron fragments, killing and wounding the surrounders of the King, and wounding himself so grievously that, when he was borne to his tent and knew how near his dissolution was, he strictly charged his chiefs to storm the fort before the breath should leave his body.

"When 'Isá Khán Hájib (or Chief Chamberlain) came out and told his brother-warriors that it was the order of the dying Sháh that the fort should be surrounded and stormed, on they rushed like ants or locusts, by the time of the afternoon prayer, taking the castle, putting all the infidels to the sword, and sending all of them to hell."

Still showing signs of such magnanimity as bigoted Islámites have but seldom displayed, the "Tiger King" would fain have allowed the encompassed and valiant Rájá Kirát Singh to break loose, and, although he was taken, he was admitted to quarter by the moribund vanquisher of Sultán Humáyún.

Last scene of all, to quote the "Tárikh-i-Shír-Sháhí," "On the 10th Rabíu-l-awwal, in the year of the Departure of the Prophet from Mecca 952 [which corresponds with May in the year of our Lord 1545], Shír Sháh went from the hostel of this world to rest in the mansion of happiness, and ascended peacefully from his sub-lunary abode to the heavens above."

XLV.

A MILD WAY OF INSURING THE PUNISHMENT OF A CRIMINAL.

Now it was the custom of the Mughals, should anyone amongst them have committed any crime deserving of death, should he not be condemned to undergo that penalty on the spot, to send him to the wars, so that if he were destined to be slain he might as well fall in battle; or they sent him as an envoy to rebel chiefs, thinking that there would be small likelihood of his escaping unscathed from their hands.

Sometimes he was ordered to some hot region where pestilential winds prevailed; and it was for such a reason that the obnoxious Balaktigín, or Bilkátigín, was despatched on an embassy to Egypt and Syria.

Now it appears to Il Musannif that this custom has not died out, but has been practised in more modern days, for Britain sometimes sends her consuls to Fernando Po and to Zanzíbár, which are not the most salubrious localities on the face of the earth.

XLVI.

AMÍR TAIMÚR AT DEHLÍ.

One of the most terrible scourges with which it has at different epochs pleased the Almighty to afflict this earth, from the days of Attila the Hun down to the "little Corsican," was undoubtedly the "Lame Chief Taimúr," or, as we call him, "Tamerlane."

Two centuries had his people dwelt in Kesh by Samarkand, where the Persian and Turkí tongues mingled. Grandson of the chief of the tribe of Berlás, he claimed descent from Janjíz Khán. No heathen, as his forefather had been, but a Musulmán, he equalled, if he did not surpass, his ancestor in barbarity.

A barbarian raider on a giant scale, he never lent his mind to the retention of the countries which had been devastated by his hordes and rendered uninhabitable by his sanguinary savagery. His was a torrent of carnage, which, passing with lightning rapidity over fair and fertile countries, suddenly receded, leaving a wilderness behind. Certain portions of his empire did, indeed, remain to such of his descendants as were gifted with the science of founding governments of Asiatic duration, but the remaining territories only exemplified that—

> Where the Tartar's hoof hath trod,
> The verdure flies the bloody sod.

Having crushed Persia and the countries beyond the Oxus, and made deserts of Tartary, Georgia, and Mesopotamia, together with parts of Russia and Siberia, news reached him that the empire of the Tughlak dynasty in Hindústán had been broken up into many fractions under the boy Mahmúd, the last of the race of the son of the Turkí slave of Ghíásu-d-dín.

His avant-coureur and grandson, Núru-d-dín, had

captured Multán after an arduous six months' siege, and the bold governor only fled by water with his family and treasures when the tidings of the approach of Amír Taimúr in person reached his ears.

By this time the Tartars of Núru-d-dín had lost most of those hardy steeds, which, although they had borne their riders safely across the plains and mountains of Upper Asia, were fatally stricken by the intense heat and absence of forage which prevailed on the shores of the Indus.

Meanwhile the Amír had marched, in the year of the Christian Era 1398, through Kábul to the confluence of the Jamú and Chináb, where stood the fortalice of Tulamba. There the miserable inhabitants of the town were ruthlessly massacred in spite of their submission. After collecting provisions for his troops and defeating the Gakkar chieftain Jassarat, at the town of Sháhnawáz, he, in true Tartar-fashion, consumed with fire the grain he could not transport with him, and made his way across the Biyás into a rich and fertile country soon destined to share the fate of so many other lands.

In the meantime Núr Muhammad was in the last straits, and invested in Multán by the enraged natives of the surrounding districts; but Taimúr delayed not to rescue his grandson.

At Adjúdin he relented for a while, and spared *some* of the inhabitants because their city contained the shrine of the sainted and poetical Faríd; but at Batner, in spite of an accepted capitulation, the streets were reddened with the blood of the people of Díbálpúr and of other towns who had fled there for shelter, until, at last, the natives, rendered desperate by such unsparing cruelty, died sword in hand, after having slain their wives and children.

On marched "the Fire-brand of the World," carrying rapine and slaughter through Surustí, Fathábád, and every town on his road to the pleasant town of Kaithal near Sámána, where he joined those of his detachments which had in the meantime desolated and ravaged the entire provinces of Multán and Lahore.

For some distance before reaching Sámána he had found no one to slaughter, because all had fled before his merciless arms; skeletons only marked the road of Taimúr the Tartar, as the skeletons of camels indicate the road through an Arab or African waste.

When he reached that famous town of Pánípat—distant but seventy-eight English miles from Dehlí, and now as happy under the mild rule of Great Britain as it was miserable in olden days, because, situated as it was on the great military route between Western Asia, Afghánistán, and the Panjáb on one side, and Central and Eastern Hindústán, it was, times innumerable, the battle-field of those who struggled on its now fertile plains for supremacy in Hindústán—Taimúr caused his soldiers to don their quilted sword-proof vestments of war, crossed the Jamná, and, storming the fort of Láúní, put the garrison to the sword.

After a skirmish, in which he routed the Hindústánís, he beheaded one of their chief nobles who had fallen into his hands, and deliberately butchered all the captives of his onward march from the Indus.

Policy was the motive of this fiendish deed, which gained for him very worthily the title of Halák Khán, "the Destroying Chief"; and as some hundred thousand human beings passed into eternity that day by his order, he had well earned the name by an action which surpassed even all *his* previous ferocious atrocities.

And here we may pause for a while to remark that the true character of this extraordinary man may be better gathered from his own plain Turkí autobiography than from the histories of his sycophants. In it, whilst he owns himself capable of the vilest intrigue and grossest perfidy, he prides himself on the virtues of goodness and sincerity, and mingles cant and hypocrisy with genuine superstition and devotion. Only Taimúr could have dictated that book, which discloses all the skill of a wily politican, gifted with courage, prudence, and address, joined to a thorough knowledge of mankind, and a Machiavellian ability to play with their weaknesses.

On the 5th of Jamádí-ul-awwal the Amír forded the Jamna, unopposed, with his Mughals, and encamped in and about that portion of Dehlí known as Fírúzábád.

Here he formed a singular breastwork of buffaloes, whom he fastened together with ropes in front of his troops; and when the army of Dehlí, commanded by Sultán Muhammad Tughlak and his minister Ikbál, together with 120 armoured elephants, advanced to meet him, his veteran squadrons, known as "the Heroes of Chagatai," hurled back at the first onset the huge animals which headed the army of Hindústán. Wounded by thrust of spear and sword-cut, they turned shrieking round against those of their own side, and carried confusion and terror with them, scattering the troops of Muhammad, until the crowd of fugitives found shelter within the walls of Dehlí.

Not trusting to his fortress, Muhammad fled that very night with coward-speed towards Gújrát, whilst Ikbál hid his diminished head elsewhere.

Some of Taimúr's cavaliers overtook the Sultán, slew several of his retainers, and seized his two infant sons, Saifu-d-dín and Khudádád, but the monarch himself escaped from their pitiless hands.

Taimúr at first affected leniency. The great men of Dehlí crowded into the camp of the "Conqueror," who received their submission, together with large contributions, and promised them protection.

On the following Friday he was proclaimed Emperor in all the mosques of the city, and on the 16th day of Jamádí-ul-awwal—black day for the unhappy citizens!—he ordained that guards should be placed at the gates to prevent egress, and that the magistrates and scribes should take note of the possessions and wealth of every inhabitant with a view to a thorough spoliation of the place.

A rumour spreading that certain of the Dehlí nobles had retired to their houses and refused to disburse their share of the ransom, the Amír sent troops into the city, nominally to aid the magistrates in carrying out his orders; but when he did so he well knew what the result would be, for no one was better aware than he of the habitual ferocity and insubordination of his troops.

The Mughals immediately spread in every direction, and plunder and outrage ruled supreme for five terrible days. Then the "Firebrand," who had been celebrating his recent victory in camp, saw the flames bursting out from every quarter of the city; and the Hindús, exasperated at their own maltreatment and at the pollution of their wives and daughters, following, their ancient custom, slaying the latter, setting fire to their dwellings, and then for a time seeking death, sword in hand, amidst the ranks of their oppressors.

But the despair of the wretched Hindús of Dehlí only had the effect of nerving the Mughals to fiercer measures; the entire army of Taimúr rushed pell-mell into the city, hacking and hewing until the streets became all but impassable from the bodies of the slain.

Then the Hindús threw aside their weapons and held out their heads to their butchers; scores, and even hundreds, allowed themselves to be driven along by a single Tartar; had they, ten to one as they were, courageously continued their onset on the Mughals, who were dispersed on every side in their greed of spoil, the invaders would have fared ill; but, as is the fashion of their nation, the first wild outburst of wrath and vengeance past, they subsided into stolid and apathetic indifference to their fate.

The greater part of the ill-gained plunder was left in the hands of the murderers, and the Amír reserved for his own use only the elephants and the regalia.

The small, lean, ill-favoured Mughal savage had still, however, some appreciation for the unequalled architecture of Hind; for when he made his public entry into Dehlí after the massacre, he was so enchanted with the beauty of the mosque erected by Sháh Fírúz, that he ordered that a sufficient number of stone-cutters and masons should be pressed in Dehlí to build a similar mosque in his own Samarkand.

Laden with plunder, the Amír now resolved to return home, which he did after storming the fort of Mírat, now a great cantonment of the troops of the Empress of India, and putting its garrison to the sword. As was his wont, slaughter, fire, and rapine marked his road. From the mountains of Sewálik and Jamú he marched onwards; the Gakkar Prince of Lahore was captured and beheaded; Khizr, afterwards King, became his deputy in Multán, Díbálpúr, and Lahore, and passing through Kábul, he at length sought repose at Samarkand.

The "Zafar-námah" of Maulána Sharafu-d-dín tells, that when, on the 3rd of Rabí'u-s-sání, Amír Jahán Sháh and others represented to Taimúr that from the time he crossed the Indus a hundred thousand Hindú prisoners, more or less, had been taken, and that these "ghabrs" and idol-worshippers were kept in camp, it was to be feared that on the day of battle with the forces of Dehlí they might join the enemy—this opinion was confirmed by the joy which the prisoners had exhibited when Mallú Khán attacked the Imperial forces—Taimúr considered the point, and deeming the advice of his officers to be wise, he gave orders for all the Hindú prisoners to be put to death. Everyone who neglected to comply with this command was to be executed, and his wives, children, and goods were to become the property of the informer. In pursuance of this order 100,000 infidel Hindús were put to the sword. Mauláná Násiru-d-dín, a most distinguished ecclesiastic, had fifteen Hindús in his train, and he who had never caused a sheep to be slaughtered was obliged to have these fifteen Hindús killed. Taimúr also issued an order, "after"—as he says in his own memoirs, (known as the "Malfuzát-i-Taimúrí")—"the whole of these vile idolaters had been sent to hell," that one man out of every ten should be left in camp to guard the wives and children of the prisoners and the captured cattle.

Now when the great chief of the Mughals had overcome Dehlí, he captured the strong fortalice of Mírat by the skill of his engineers, and won a battle near the Ganges, where, although suffering at the time from severe rheumatic pains, he swam his horsemen up to the boats of the Hindús who had assembled to oppose his passage at the fords, and there slew many of them, sending the infidels, as he relates in true, unadulterated Musulmán fashion, "through water to the fires of hell"; then, after winning three battles in one day and conquering the hills of the Siwálik range with great overflow of Hindú blood and incalulable amount of spoil, he came before the town of Nagarkot, now known as Kángrá, in which the compiler of this work once passed an entire year (1849) whilst on duty with a detachment. From the summit of a lofty mountain, and seated amongst the slaughtered carcases of the infidels, Taimúr watched the exploits of "his hungry, sharp-eyed wolves, who, as they fell upon the fox-like heathens, dyed their weapons in the blood of these wretches until the sanguine streams ran down the valley."

The only living things that annoyed the savage

Mughal with impunity, and even treated him with contumely, were those holy animals the monkeys; "they entered the camps," says Taimúr in his "Malfuzát-i-Taimúrí," "from the jungles and woods, both by night and day, and laid their claws upon whatever they could find to eat, and carried it off before the face of the men; at night they stole their little articles and curiosities."

The compiler begs to add that his own experience of the Kángrá monkeys impressed him with the fact that they had not abandoned the evil customs of their forbears, for they were as unscrupulous in his time in appropriating the food and property of the red-coated Britons as their ancestors had been in annexing the belongings of the Tartar hordes.

Taimúr's mode of conversion was most convincing to those who had any love of life; but not only in his day, but throughout the whole of the lengthened period (during which but a few sparkling examples of good and just governments are to be met with) during which the "Religion of the Sword" held sway over the cowering majority of the Hindú races, there were not unfrequently heroic men amongst the idol-worshippers who, like Lord Byron's "Prisoner of Chillon,"

> Perished at the stake,
> For tenets they would not forsake.

The Rájá of Jammú was not disposed to become a

martyr, and when he had been inveigled into an ambush by the troops of the invader, and brought in wounded, he was tended in brotherly fashion, as Taimúr remarks, "for the sake of the ransom-money."

During his convalescence, by "*hopes, fears, and threats,* he was brought to see the beauty of Islám; he repeated the Kalimah, or declaration of faith, and ate the flesh of the cow, which is an abomination to his countrymen. This obtained him great honour and the protection of the Emperor."

Thus does a Hindústání scribe unflatteringly paint the Mughals: "There were," says he, writing of the reception of an envoy by Taimúr, "more than a thousand Tartar infidels and warriors of other tribes, riding on camels, great commanders in battle, all with steel-like bodies, clothed in cotton, with faces of fire, with caps of sheepskin and shorn heads. Their eyes were so narrow and piercing that they might have bored a hole in a brazen vessel. Their stink was more horrible than their colour; their faces were set on their bodies as if they had no neck; their cheeks resembled soft leathern bottles, full of wrinkles and knots; their noses extended from cheek to cheek, and their mouths from cheek-bone to cheek-bone; their nostrils resembled rotten graves, and from them the hair descended to the lips; their moustaches were of extravagant length; they had but scanty beards about their chins; their chests, of a colour half black, half white, were so covered with lice that they looked like sesame growing on a bad soil; their whole bodies, indeed, were covered with these insects, and their skin was as rough-grained as shagreen leather, fit only to be converted into shoes. They devoured dogs and pigs with their nasty teeth."

XLVII.

SULTÁN BÁBAR AT PÁNÍPAT.

On the 17th of November, A.D. 1525, when bluff King Hal ruled England, memorable day in the annals of Hindústán, Sultán Bábar set forth from Pesháwar on his last invasion of that Peninsula, with but 12,000 followers who had fought and bled with their chief on many a stricken field, but the courage of the valiant Mughal and of his trusty soldiers quailed not before the arduous task which ambition had marked out for him.

The rushing Atak and Chináb presented no obstacles to his rapid march. Concentrating his troops at Siálkot, and unawed by the defeat sustained by his ally 'Alim Khán near Dehlí at the hands of the Afgháns of Sultán Ibráhím, his detachments scattered themselves over the Panjáb, and he mastered the forts of Kalanúr (between the Rávi and the Biyás) and Milwat.

The chief of the latter place, Daulat Khán, had formerly received many benefits from the Sultán, but had revolted and swaggeringly shown himself in public armed with two swords, with which he boasted he would annihilate the Mughal.

His courage, however, cooled marvellously when the tidings of the return of Bábar reached him: he took refuge in the lower range of the Himálayas in fear of his life; and when he received a safe-conduct and presented himself in humble guise before the Sultán, the only revenge the hero allowed himself over his fallen foe was to cause him to wear his two swords suspended round his neck for a short time.

He was then gently reproached and reinstated in the command of his tribe and in his possessions. This was a great stroke of policy; for Daulat Khán, from having been the trusted ally of the Lodís, now became the staunch adherent of the invader.

After sending troops in pursuit of another traitor Ghází Khán, to use his own words, "he placed his foot in the stirrup of resolution and his hand on the reins of confidence in God," and marched against Sultán Ibráhím, the son of Sultán Iskandar, the son of Sultán Bahlol Lodí Afghán, in whose possession the throne of Dehlí and the dominions of Hindústán were, and whose army in the field was said to amount to a hundred thousand foot and nearly a thousand elephants.

Yet Bábar feared not to confront this prodigious

multitude with a tenth of their number of his own countrymen and some uncertain allies. At last Ambálah, now a great cantonment of British troops, was reached, and Bábar's young son Humáyun, who commanded the right wing of the army, drew the first blood by defeating Ibráhím's general Hamíd Khán in a sharp skirmish. It is pitiful here to observe the massacres of the wounded and mutilation of the dead, only too frequently ordered by this comparatively chivalric and generous descendant of Taimúr. On this occasion half the prisoners were decapitated, and Bábar coolly relates in his memoirs that he "ordered Ustád Kulí Khán and the matchlock-men to shoot the remainder as *an example.*"

It was truly no compliment to the Russians when the Great Napoleon uttered the celebrated "*Grattez le Russe et vous trouverez le Tartare*"; but General Kaufmann's recent exploits in Central Asia, although they did not quite come up to the mark of the pyramids of skulls with which Janjíz, Taimúr, and even Bábar marked the track of their destroying hordes, were sufficiently savage to prove the justice of Napoleon's estimate of the character of the Muscovites of this nineteenth century of the Christian Era.

After some preliminary skirmishes, the advantages of which generally remained with the Mughals, Sultán Bábar marched on to Pánípat on the 30th of the month of Jamádu-l-akhir.

Fortifying his position to the left of the town with breast-works, trenches, and abattis of trees, and leaving open spaces at the distance of every bow-shot to allow the troops to sally forth at need, he linked his gun-carriages together after the manner of the Turks, whose reputation as artillerists was at that time very high in the East, and posted his matchlock-men behind them.

Determined as Bábar was, he found much reason for discouragement, less in the presence of an enemy whose forces greatly outnumbered his than in the tremor and alarm which pervaded his own troops.

"Trepidation and fear," says this warlike philosopher, "are always unbecoming. Whatsoever Almighty God has decreed from all eternity cannot be reversed; though, at the same time, I cannot greatly blame them; they had some reason, for they had come two or three months' journey from their own country; we had to engage in arms strange nations whose language we did not understand, and who did not understand ours."

Bábar's great source of confidence under these perilous circumstances lay in his knowledge of the ineptitude and meanness of his adversary Ibráhín, whose cruel misgovernment and avarice had alienated so many of the best supporters of his family. Daulat Khán, the double traitor, had written to him that "his own bad actions and not he (Daulat Khán) had brought the Mughals into India."

The constant vacillations of the Lodí Emperor and his utter want of generalship, stood the Mughals in good stead. During a week's stay in their fortified camp at Pánípat, all their insulting demonstrations could not draw Ibráhím into an attack on their position for some time, but encouraged by the repulse of the Mughál warriors in a mismanaged night-attack, the Hindústánís took heart of grace early on the following morning and advanced in battle array.

Bábar, bracing on his helmet and armour, mounted his horse at the old Sarái of Garaunda, which is still in existence and in tolerable condition, whilst Sultán Ibráhím chose his position about a league to the east of Pánípat.

The latter, whose astrologers, "aware," says the chronicle, "of their master's impending doom," had all deserted his camp, attempted at the last moment by conciliatory speeches and large gifts to reclaim his disaffected adherents, but they had little confidence either in his words or deeds, and went half-hearted into one of the fiercest battles on record, and one which proved a turning-point in the history of India.

Stern Bábar, with his right wing commanded by the fledgling Humáyun, whose deeds in his early days much remind us of the conduct of our own "Black Prince" at Cressy, and his left ordered by Muhammad Sultán Mírzá and other chiefs, prepared for the onset.

On came the Afgháns, boldly at first, but somewhat hesitating when in sight of the formidable intrenched camp of the Mugháls; of this untimely hesitation the skilful Mughál general took instant advantage, wheeling strong bodies of his men round the enemies' flank and attacking their rear, he simultaneously advanced both his right and left divisions against their front.

Now the battle fairly joined, and the Mughál archers committed frightful havoc. Mustafa the Osmánlí cannoneer, handled his rude artillery in a manner which created consternation amongst the Hindústánís, who, nevertheless, contested the victory with indomitable obstinacy; even the weak Ibráhím when he saw the tide turn against him, refused to listen to the counsels of flight given him by his friend Mahmúd Khán.

There is something very chivalrous and kingly in his last words; they in some measure redeem an otherwise despicable reputation from the slur of utter contempt.

"O! Mahmúd Khán," said the falling monarch, "it is a disgrace for kings to fly from the field of battle. Look here! my nobles, my companions, my well-wishers and friends have partaken of the cup of martyrdom; one has fallen there, another here; where then, can I go? My horse's legs are dyed with blood up to his chest. Whilst I was King I governed the empire as I pleased; now perfidious Fortune has sided with the Mugháls, what pleasure is there in life? It is better that I should be like my friends, in the dust and blood."

Spurring into the midst of the enemy at the head of some 5,000 horse, he fell fighting to the last.

By noon the Afghán-Indian army was utterly dispersed, from fifteen to sixteen thousand corpses strewed the battle-field.

A savage follower of Bábar named Tákir Tabarí, having been the first to discover the dead body of Ibráhím amidst the heaps of the slain, cut his head off and brought it to his master, but the Sultán who honoured his brave adversary, caused him to be honourably interred with due pomp, and erected a fitting mausoleum over his remains on the spot where he had been found.

Such was the decisive fall of the Lúdí Afgháns, after having been rulers of Hindústán during seventy years; the remainder, abandoning their dwellings and their wealth, sought refuge in Bengal.

Keenly alive to the main chance, as became one of the truly rapacious Tartar brood, Bábar, on the very day of the victory, despatched Prince Humáyun to secure the city and treasures of Agra, and sent Mahdí Khwájá on a similar errand to Dehlí.

Marching himself in leisurely fashion to the neighbourhood of Dehlí, and relieving himself from the fatigues of his late marches and campaign, he finished the third day after the battle, like a jovial Sultán as he was, by retiring to a boat on the Jumná and there indulging in strong drink in company with some other festive and boon companions.

On the Friday the Khutba was read in his name in the mosques of Dehlí, and thus began the reign of the first Mughál Emperor of Hindústán, the first of the offspring of Amír Taimúr who occupied that throne, which only finally departed from his degenerate descendants when the British stormers carried the faithless and blood-stained city in the year of grace eighteen hundred and fifty-seven.

XLVIII.

SULTÁN BÁBAR'S ACCOUNT OF THE LAND OF HIND.

When Sultán Bábar first conquered Hindústán in the year of grace 1525, he looked keenly around him, and a few extracts from his graphic account of his new possessions may well be given here.

"The country and towns of Hindústán," says the royal scribe, "are extremely ugly, and have a uniform and monotonous aspect; the greater part of it consists of level plains, its gardens have no walls, the banks of its rivers and streams, owing to the rapid torrents which descend during the rains, are worn deep into the channel, and are generally difficult to cross. In many places the plains are covered by a thorny brushwood to such a degree that the people of the parganas, relying on these jungles, take refuge in their almost inaccessible depths beyond the reach of the tax-gatherer. Except the great rivers, there is but little running water in Hind, now and then there are pools and lakes, but all these cities and countries chiefly procure their water from wells and tanks, in which it is collected during the rains. In Hindústán the populousness and decay of villages, and even cities, is almost the work of a moment. Large cities that have long been thickly inhabited are utterly abandoned in the course of a few hours in times of panic and invasion. Hindústán has few pleasures to recommend it. The people are not handsome, they have no idea of the charms of friendly society, of frankly meeting together, or of familiar intercourse; they have no genius, no comprehension of mind, no politeness of manner, no kindness or fellow-feeling, no ingenuity or mechanical invention in planning or executing their handicraft works, no skill or knowledge in design or architecture, they have no good horses, or meat, no grapes, or musk-lemons, no good fruits, no hot or cold water, no good food or bread in their bázárs, no baths or colleges, no candles, no torches, not even a candle-stick."

After giving this rather jaundiced view of his new Empire and its inhabitants, the Sultán comes to what, from a Muhammadan stand-point, was the root of the matter in this detested but much-coveted country.

"The chief excellency of Hindústán," he writes, "is that it is a spacious country *and abounds in gold and silver*. The climate during the rains is very pleasant; on some days it rains ten and even twenty times, and at this period inundations pour suddenly down and form rivers, even in places where at other times there is no water.

"Whilst the rains moisten the earth, the atmosphere is delightful, although too much impregnated with moisture. During the rainy season the bows of the archers become unserviceable, and not they alone, but coats of mail, books, clothes, and furniture suffer from the damp [as Il Musannif has often witnessed in swampy, jungly, and miry Gílán, in the *unfair* land of Irán]. There is pleasant weather enough in the winter and summer seasons, as well as during the monsoon, but then the north wind blows and dust-storms prevail. On the approach of the 'barsát,' or 'season of the rains,' these dust-storms herald its arrival, and are called 'áudhí' by the natives. When the 'Bull' and the 'Twins' constellations are in the ascendant, the heat is bearable and far less than that of Balkh and Kandahár."

"Another convenience of Hindústán," says Bábar, with more inconsistency than we should have expected from a monarch of such genius and observation, but who had so recently penned such a disparaging account of his Hindú subjects, "is that workmen of every kind are obtainable at all times. There is always a set ready to whom the same employment and trade have been handed down from father to son."

In the Zafar-námah of Sharífu-d-dín, Yazdí, it is mentioned as a wonder that when Amír Taimúr was erecting the Sangín (or Ponderous) mosque, stone-cutters from Media, Persia, and India did daily work there, "and when I (Bábar) dwelt in Agra, men who came from no other city were daily busy at my building-work to the number of 680 persons."

Besides describing his countrymen and contemporaries with such minuteness and semblance of reality that they come before us as did the English of former days in the graphic pages of Thomas Babington Macaulay, it is charming to trace the fine character of the royal author, whose affectionate disposition never varied during his many trials and throughout his adventurous life; the same easy and sociable disposition with which he began his career, and the same refined taste, were neither blunted nor diminished by his subsequent rise to the Imperial dignity.

"It is a relief," says one of his translators, in the pompous coldness of Asiatic history, "to find a King who can tell that he wept for the playmate of his childhood, and one who can take an interest in the welfare of his mother, his relatives, and his friends."

In writing on State matters to his confidant and friend Khwája Kalán, then at Kábul, amidst many amusing anecdotes regarding their mutual friends, he says, "Drinking was a pleasant thing with our old friends and companions; but now that you have only Shír Ahmad and Haidar Kulí to drink with, it can be no great sacrifice to leave off wine."

So, although the Great Mughál loved a social glass, he evidently abhorred and detested *solitary* drunkards, but, in spite of many attempts at reformation, he thoroughly proved the truth of the old French saying, "*Qui a bú, boira,*" "Who has drunk, will drink".

Many a drinking-bout do his memoirs record, and his happy relations of such scenes are not the most unpleasant or unreadable portions of this autobiography. Selecting for such indulgences a shady grove, a hill overlooking an agreeable landscape, or floating lazily down the current of a stream—recitations, repartee, and song enlivened the hearts of Sultán Bábar and his men, even when they had but recently emerged from a battle-field reeking with carnage.

Thus does this royal toper recount one of these rather undignified orgies which was held in the very teeth of dangerous adversaries:—

"We continued drinking until the sun began to decline, and then we put our feet into the stirrups.

Those of our convivial party were utterly drunk. Saiyyid Kásim [a nice descendant of the Prophet!] was so far gone that two of his servants had to support him as he sat in the saddle, and brought him with difficulty into camp."

Dost Muhammad Bákir was so entirely besotted that, although anxious friends soused him unhesitatingly with that fluid which was so dear to the late Father Matthew, he could not be got on horseback. Just then, as ill-luck would have it, a body of savage Afghán horsemen made their appearance, and one of the most inebriated of Bábar's chosen companions, Amír Muhammad Tarkhún, gravely told them that as he felt totally incapable of self-defence under the circumstances, he would feel greatly obliged to his comrades if they would cut off his head and carry it beyond the risk of Afghan desecration and defilement of the slain. Somehow, however, they packed up this valiant and fearless toper on his horse and led him out of danger.

To be drunk four times within the twenty-four hours was an ordinary achievement.

"Once," says the jovial warrior-king, "we passed the night amidst our cups in the tent; then we felt drunk and went to sleep." This happened at that same Istálif which was stormed in the year of our Lord 1841 by the avenging British legions under Sir John McCaskill.

Coming thence to Bahzádí, and unsatisfied with the intoxicating electuary or "pick-me-up" of Májún, which he had swallowed on the road, Sháh Bábar and his boon companions ensconced themselves beneath a pleasant grove, surrounded by bright ripe harvest-fields, and there imbibed until even-song.

In or about A.D. 1527, after much very free-living of the same description, the Lord of Upper Hind was seized with contrition, and abandoned for a time that excessive indulgence which undoubtedly shortened the life of as brave and clement a Bayard as was ever written of in Eastern chronicle; but he was an Asiatic after all. In his wars in Hind and Afghánistán his prisoners were butchered ruthlessly in his presence, and pyramids of their fleshless heads were left behind to commemorate his victories and to intimidate possible opponents. The ground in front of the royal tent was drenched in blood and strewn with quivering carcases.

When an unsuccessful attempt to poison him had been discovered, his official taster was hacked to pieces, his cook was skinned alive, and the understrappers of the kitchen were crushed into a jelly by elephants.

Since his eleventh birthday he had never kept the fast of Ramazán in one locality, and the time which he did not pass in war or journeys was taken up by the chase or other distractions.

When his health was on the decline he rode over

the 120 miles which divide Kálpí from Agra in forty-eight hours, and twice did he swim his horse through the Ganges, as had always been his wont with every stream he had ever encountered.

And here we leave the stalwart Mughál, who fell sick in the month of Rajab in the year of "the Departure" 936, and died and was buried in a sepulchre in Kábul in the course of the following year. Fifty years of age was he when he ended his varied reign of eight-and-thirty years, and on his tomb was inscribed the date of his death.

بهشت روزی اش باد "May heaven be his lot!"

Perhaps the relatives, the widows, and the orphans of Hindú hecatombs did not share this opinion.

XLIX.

ACUTE MAKHDÚMU-L-MULK.

The above worthy could not see the necessity, for religious reasons, of going on prilgrimage to Mecca and Madínah, and even maintained that to do so was sinful, "for," said he, "the only two ways to the shrines lie through Persia and Gujarát. By the former the Kizilbáshes (or red-headed Persian Shías) din into the ears of the orthodox Sunní profane abuse of the Khalífah 'Umr, and by the other route the Portuguese infidels compel the True Believer to give a written engagement, stamped with the portraits of the Virgin Mary and of Jesus Christ—upon whom be peace," piously remarks 'Abdu-l-Kádir Badáúni, who, in common with the rest of the sons of Islám, past and present, allowed the prophetic mission but denied the divinity of the Saviour of mankind, and deemed portraiture idolatry.

In fact, as Il Musannif gathers from Portuguese writers of that period, a journey by sea to Jiddah was one of no ordinary peril, inasmuch as the too-confiding Musulmáns who accepted and paid heavily for the passports of the Sons of the Cross too often discovered, ere they reached their journey's end, that these documents were "letters of Bellerophon."

"The owner of this ship," wrote the Portuguese official, "is a very wicked Moor, and is fair booty for the first of our nation who may come across him."

Now, Makhdúmu-l-Mulk was as sordid as he was wealthy, and to avoid the payment of the percentage for alms to the needy ordained by Muhammadan law (a sort of income-tax, in fact), used to consign his property yearly to his wife, and then take it back again when the danger of taxation was over.

"Such tricks did he play," relates his unfriendly biographer, "that even Jews would be ashamed to perpetrate them."

L.

THE DEATH OF DÁÚD, THE AFGHÁN CHIEF OF THE EAST.

Now when defeat fell on the Afgháns at the hands of Khán Jahán, the princely Dáúd of Bengal was borne into the presence of his conqueror, who at first took compassion on him and quenched his thirst with water from his own flask. Desirous of sparing so fine a youth, he would fain have done so, but at length, yielding to the pressure put on to him by the other chieftains, he ordered his execution, which was carried out with a want of dexterity most unusual in the butchering East, for when, as the annalist 'Abdu-lla composedly remarks, Khán Jahán ordered them "to relieve his body from the weight of his head," the head was hacked off by slow degrees, to the great torment of the unfortunate Dáúd, and then, when stuffed with straw and anointed with perfumes, sent as a token of success to Akbar the King.

LI.

THE VALIANT GROCER-RÁJÁ HÍMÚ.

When Muhammad Sháh Súr 'Adilí, or 'Adil Sháh, had compassed the throne by the slaughter of his boy-nephew, son of the late Salím Sháh, he chose the "bakkál" Hímú, the idolater, to be his minister; yet although as mean in stature as in birth, this Hindú propped up the tottering State and prevented for a time, by force of ability, the fall of an empire the gross and filthy lusts and excesses of whose head were fast leading it towards destruction.

Profuse waste of treasure and general misrule led to the loss of both Dehlí and Agra, which remained in the hands of his own relation 'Ibráhím Súr. The country of the Five Rivers fell away from him, and he had no sovereignty left but in the eastern possessions of his family; even there he would have lost everything but for the sturdy Hímú, who, unawed even by the tidings of the return of Sháh Humáyun from the west, totally routed Muhammad Súr, the usurper in Bengal, and slew him; and when news was brought that the Mughál king had died through an accident shortly after the recovery of his ancient territories, Hímú lost no time, after placing his puppet-monarch Sháh 'Adil in the strong fortress of Chunár, in marching to face the young Sultán Akbar. At first Fortune smiled pleasantly and promisingly on the Grocer-General and Mayor of the Palace, whose supreme mastery over so many stubborn and fierce Afghán chiefs was little short of the miraculous, considering his heathen origin. Crowds of his co-religionists flocked to his standard; Gwálíar and Agra were conquered by him, and he advanced to and encamped near old Dehlí in three divisions. At first the Afgháns of Rájá Hímú were discomfited by the shafts of the Mughál archers, but the fight was restored by the valour of the undaunted Hímú, who broke through his opponents so thoroughly that they left the field in hot haste, and abandoned, besides incalculable spoil of every kind, 160 elephants and more than 1,000 Arab horses.

These spoils Hímú reserved not for himself, but for his covetous but valiant Afgháns, whose greed of gain thus made them his steadfast partisans.

So, assuming the airs of a sovereign prince, the ex-shopkeeper, with the consent of his followers, raised the Imperial canopy in Dehlí, and caused coin to be struck in his name.

Whilst appointing his own governors and whilst he was *de facto* master of the land, he thus hypocritically addressed his effeminate tool and nominal monarch 'Adil Sháh :—

"Your slave, by the royal fortune, has routed the army of the Mugháls, which was firm as a wall of iron; but I hear that the son of Humáyun is advancing with a powerful force against Dehlí. For this reason I have kept the horses and elephants of the Mughál in order that I might face the enemy and hinder him from reaching Dehlí."

And poor 'Adil Sháh was comforted by these

deceitful assertions. When princely Akbar heard of the defeat and downheartedness of the Chagatai nobles who had fled before the skill and bravery of the infidel Hímú, he marched with his able tutor Bairám Khán to Sarhund, and enlisted supporters as he proceeded.

At Thánísar his army was found to be 26,000 strong, and both he and Hímú pitched their tents on the blood-stained fields of Pánípat. Then relying, after the superstitious custom of his race, on the favourable predictions of a madman of the camp, Ahmad Bey, who had prognosticated certain victory to the Mugháls from the inspection of the blade-bone of a sheep, he gathered his chieftains together and bade them be of good cheer, did this boy of ten.

On the third day Hímú came forward to the contest, seated in a jewelled handa and with the royal standards unfurled, whilst Bairám Khán marshalled his men of Chagatai in battle-array.

At the first onslaught the courageous and daring Hindú bore down the inferior numbers of his opponents, until he was stricken in the forehead with an arrow, and the flight of his elephant, as has almost invariably been the result of the fall of an Oriental chief, turned the tide of victory to the side of Prince Akbar.

Then the wounded warrior was brought before the young king, who disdained to shed the blood of his heroic and prostrate foe, although strongly pressed thus fortunately to initiate his reign, and acquire the title of Ghází by the cold-blooded slaughter of the valiant unbeliever, by his stern tutor Bairám.

Bairám then murdered the captive with his own hands, and these events befell on the 5th day of November in the year of our Lord 1556.

LII.

SULTÁN AKBAR, THE INFALLIBLE.

In the year 987 after "the Departure" a declaration was made under the signets of the most learned of the age, which had for its object to establish the superiority of the "Just Leader" over the "Chief Lawyer of the Church," and to make him the chief authority in many questions, both religious and political, and this declaration was thus worded :—

"We have agreed that a Sultán-i-'adil is higher than a Mujtahid, and that the Sultán of Islám, the refuge of the faith, the leader of the faithful, the shadow of God upon earth, 'Abu-l-Fath, Jalálu-d-dín, Muhammad Akbar-i-Ghází (whose kingdom may God perpetuate) is a most just, wise, and God-fearing King. Therefore, if there be variance of opinion amongst the expounders of the law in matters of religion, and the unerring judgment of His Majesty should incline to one opinion, and issue his decree for the benefit of his subjects, we hereby consent that such a decision shall be binding upon us and upon the rest of the nation.

"Opposition to his decree shall involve damnation in the world to come and loss of land and living on this earth; and this document, written with the best intentions for the glory of God and the spreading of Islám, has been signed by us, the Chief Priests and Lawyers, in the month of Rajab, A.H. 987."

So Sultán Akbar became *infallible*, long before Pius the Ninth of Rome, and as the Pope of Muhammadanism, he adopted the declaration of faith "There is no God but God, and Akbar is God's representative," and was a downright Free-thinker. Listening to the opinions of everyone, especially of those who were not Muhammadans, he concluded that truth could not be confined to one single religion or to a creed like that of Islám, which was of comparatively recent date. He heard the Pandits and Brahmans of the Hindús, and the Padres or missionaries from Europe, with equal attention, and even ordered Shaikh Abu-l-Fazl to translate the gospel of the Christians into the vernacular of Hind.

To propitiate the Hindús he also forbade the slaughter of bulls, alleging as his reason that learned physicians had represented their flesh as productive of divers diseases and as difficult of digestion.

LIII.

HOW SULTÁN AKBAR TUSSLED WITH A TIGER.

Now, during the holy fast of Ramazán, in the year of the Hijreh 975, the Sultán quitted Ajmír and went his way through the Mewát jungles towards Agra, and being confronted by a giant-tiger, the animal was speedily slain by the arrows of his guards.

But so facile a victory did not meet the views of a monarch ever ready to set the example of extreme daring to his followers, and he ordained that in future, should such an event occur, no missiles were to be discharged without his express order.

He and his retinue had made but little further progress when another and still more powerful and furious quadruped of the same species dashed into their path and rushed savagely towards the Emperor, who coolly descended from his steed and aimed steadily at the beast with his matchlock; the animal, being only slightly injured, continued his onward career, but steady Akbar brought him for a time to the ground with a second shot. Up rose the striped enemy of men once more, and threw himself on the stalwart Afghán of Kandahár, 'Adil Muhammad, who was dragged to the ground by the savage brute.

Overpowered as he was, the Afghán thrust his hand and arm into the mouth of his adversary, and sought to draw his dagger and stab him in the belly, but the handle of the weapon was so tightly fixed in its sheath that it would not come forth, and the beast gnawed the flesh of the hand which he held in his mouth. Still another effort, and the dagger was drawn, and plunged repeatedly into the body of the tiger, who was soon cut to pieces by rescuing swordsmen, who, however, wounded their comrade, unintentionally, whilst bent on saving his life.

He was not destined to survive, however, and, after passing some time on a bed of pain, he died.

LIV.

HOW THE INGRATE PRIEST ABDU-L-KÁDÍR WAS SORELY WOUNDED.

In the year of "the Departure" 979, it chanced that the calumniator of Shaikh Abu-l-Faizí was promoted to the office of judge of the districts of Kánt and Gola, which were the fiefs of Muhammad Husain Khán. He committed some impure action whilst on a pilgrimage to the shrine of the holy Shaikh Badíu-l-Hakk-wa-ud-dín Sháh Madúr, "May God sanctify his tomb," says the superstitious chronicler of this personal incident, and adds:

"This son of man, through the disposition which

he inherited from his sinful and ignorant nature (which he imbibed with the crude milk of his mother, and which is the cause of shame and reproach), and through innate darkness and ignorance (which are the sources of presumption and baseness, and which came down to him by inheritance from Father Adam), the eyes of his wisdom were covered by a film of lust, so that he committed, as was of old forewilled by Providence, a gross impropriety within that holy shrine. Since the chastisement as well as the mercy of God was upon me, I received upon earth the punishment of my sin, by his ordaining that several relatives of the girl whom I fell in love with should inflict nine sword-wounds upon my hands, head, and shoulders. They were all slight, but one penetrated the bone of my skull, thus exposing me as a brainless fellow, and another partially severed the veins of my left hand."

Pretty well for the *holy* backbiter who had been so undeservedly lauded by the unsuspicious Faizí for his *morality*, and who subsequently suffered much from his wounds, and in repentant mood vowed a pilgrimage to Mecca, which he never performed.

We can fancy we see the brethren of the ill-used damsel fiercely assaulting the sanctimonious and hypocritical breaker of the Seventh Commandment within the very precincts of a shrine venerated by all good Musulmáns.

LV.

A HIGH-FALUTING MUHAMMADAN SCRIBE.

"In the year of the Departure 587," says the annalist of the Táju-l-Ma,ásir, who, like most of his fellow-scribes, dealt largely in exaggerated hyperbole and flattery, "*the Lord of the World, the Sultán of Sultáns*, Mu'izzu-dunyá-wa-ud-dín (or Muhammad Ghorí), *in a happy moment* and under a fortunate star, departed from Ghazní, *may God protect it from misfortune.*

"Having equipped and set in order the army of Islám, *and unfurled the standards of victory and the flags of Power, trusting in the aid of the Almighty* [whose succour was invariably invoked by all True Believers, even when on the eve of the commission of the most desperate and traitorous crime], he proceeded towards Hindústán.

"When the tent of *eternal prosperity, encompassed by splendour*, arrived near Lahore, and when the *atmosphere* of that country became perfumed by the dust raised by the hoofs of his horses, *the great Sadr Kiwámu-l-Mulk, Rúhu-d-dín Hamza, who was amongst the chiefs of the country and the most famous of the State in the service of the Sublime Court* (*may Heaven surround it with increase of glory*), had met with approval, *and when from the flame of his wisdom and the light of his penetration abundant delight and perfect good fortune arose,*" he was sent on a special mission to the Hindú Rájá of Ajmír, Pithaura, and when he reached that country (to cut the matter short, for Il Musannif has already had more than enough of that redundant and exuberant verbosity which made Hasan Nizámí the admiration and model of his fellow-scribes), he found that "that man of dark understanding," Pithaura, was not to be beguiled by specious representations, and was prepared for resistance. He sent news of his recalcitrancy to the Emperor, who advanced to encounter Rái Pithaura and "his crow-faced Hindús," who were put to flight between Thanesar and Karnál, where most contests for Indian supremacy have been decided, with merciless carnage, whilst Ajmír and all its spoils fell into the hands of the Sultán. Poor Pithaura, or Prithwí Rájá, (who had in a previous campaign entirely routed his adversary, who barely escaped with his life and with the wreck of his army to the Panjáb,) whose life had at first been spared, was suspected of intrigue, "and the diamond-like sword severed the head of the abandoned wretch from his body"; whilst his son, who had contrived to win the good graces of the victor, was made his deputy in Ajmír. Then Muhammad named Kutbu-d-dín Aibak his Lord Deputy in Hind, and returned to Ghazní.

LVI.

AN UNGRATEFUL SCRIBE.

Now 'Abdu-l-Kádir was a priest of the town of Badáún, and had lived for forty years in the closest intimacy with the great minister of Sultán Akbar, Abu-l-Fazl, and his brother Shaikh Faizí, and owed many benefits both to the Emperor and to those trusty and able servants of the State; but, although the bigotry of Islám was rooted in his soul, he dissembled the intense aversion with which he invariably regarded the, in his opinion, too tolerant spirit of those benefactors whose largesses rendered him one of the wealthiest of the Court.

In a history known as the "Táríkh-i-Badáúní," he thus proceeds to maul his too confiding and liberal patrons. Speaking of Shaikh Faizí, he says :—

"As an author, he was sometimes serious, sometimes jocose, conceited, proud, and malevolent; he was full of hypocrisy, malignity, dissimulation, ambition, arrogance, and egotism. In his obstinacy and animosity he reviled the earlier and later Khalífahs and disciples, the ancestors and descendants of the Prophet, the wise and the excellent, the pious and the saintly, and, in short, Musulmáns in general, and ridiculed the principles of their faith, privately and publicly, by night and by day. His conduct was so abominable that even Jews, Christians, Hindús, Sabians, and Ghebers are considered a thousand times less odious. He acted entirely against the tenets of the Muhammadan religion; what was forbidden in that was lawful to him, and *vice versâ*.

"He composed a commentary on the Kurán, consisting entirely of letters without diacritical points, in order to obliterate his infamy, but the waters of a hundred oceans will never cleanse his stains until the Day of Judgment. He composed it in the very height of his drunkenness and impurity, and dogs were allowed to tread on every letter of it. In the same spirit of pride, stubbornness, and infidelity, he met his final doom, and in a manner which I trust no one may again see or hear of; for when the King paid him a visit on his death-bed he barked at his face like a dog, his features were swollen and his lips appeared black, so that the King observed to Abu-l-Fazl, 'What is this blackness? surely the Shaikh has been rubbing his teeth with dentifrice after the fashion of the Hindús!" "No," replied Abu-l-Fazl, "it is the stain of the blood he has been spitting."

Rather a vituperative and unworthy return for so much kindness, O incurably bigoted Abdu-l-Kádir, but not astounding in a rigid Musulmán, and still to be met with wherever the creed of the Man of Mecca flourishes.

Side by side with this unlovely picture, let us place

the conduct of the man whom he so bitterly reviles, when the crawling recipient of so much bounty once solicited a letter of recommendation from Shaikh Faizí to Sultán Akbar, who had turned his face away from the fanatical 'Abdu-l-Kádir.

Instantly acceding to the request, the Shaikh penned the following letter to the Emperor, and we now present it to our readers as one of the most charming Oriental epistolary productions on record. Thus it runs:—

"May it please your Majesty, two friends of Mullá 'Abdu-l-Kádir have arrived from Badáún in great distress and sorrow, representing that the Mullá has been for some time ill, and that in consequence of his having failed to perform the promise which he made respecting his return, the servants of the Government have treated him with great severity, and that there is no knowing what the result of it may be. They inquired, also, if the prolonged illness of the Mullá was known to your Majesty.

"Healer of the broken-hearted! Mullá 'Abdu-l-Kádir is a very able man, and is well acquainted with all the sciences usually cultivated by the Mullás of Hindústán, and he was also a pupil of my father's; your slave has been acquainted with him for nearly thirty-seven years. Besides being a person of deep learning, he is a poet, and composes elegantly in Arabic and Persian. He is not a mere imitator, but an original thinker; he also knows a little of Hindú astrology and accounts, and is not at a loss in any field of knowledge. He is acquainted with foreign as well as with native music, and can play at both the small and great games of chess; moreover, he writes a pretty good hand. Notwithstanding that he possesses all these accomplishments, he is content and entirely divested of avarice, of equable temperament, and a person of excellent morals and manners, but poor and with no fixed income; he is sincere and warm-hearted, and has every confidence in your Majesty's kindness.

"At the time the army was before Kumbhalmír, he volunteered to join it; there he did the State good service, and received a donation for his wounds. Jalál Khán Korchí, when he first introduced him at Court, said: 'I have brought a preacher to present to your Majesty, that your Majesty may be gratified.' Mír Fathu-lla also represented something respecting the Mullá's circumstances, and my worthy brother Abu-l-Fazl knows him well. But, according to the proverb, 'a grain of good-luck is better than a sackful of skill.'

"As the Court is the abode of the virtuous, I have taken the liberty to bring this destitute person to notice, and to place him before the foot of the throne as if I had been myself present. Did I not advocate his claims at this time, I should consider myself guilty of an offence against the cause of truth and justice.

"May God the Omnipotent place the slaves of the Court under the heavenly shadow of your Royal Majesty, and may He mercifully make their feet firm in pursuing the paths of rectitude and justice, and in acquiring the knowledge of truth. May He preserve your Majesty as the protector and nourisher of the helpless, the bestower of mercy, the pardoner of errors, throughout the world and all worlds, and bless you with thousands upon thousands of sources of wealth, abundance, grandeur, and felicity upon earth and in heaven. I implore this for the sake of all the pure spirits who surround the throne of grace, and the saints upon earth who join in the matutinal chorus of prayer. Amen, and amen, and amen."

Tinged though this letter may seem to the European reader with too much of the servility and adulation with which eastern courtiers invariably approach their sovereigns, we consider it a gem both in feeling and in style.

It had its effect, and much did the monster of ingratitude profit by it; for the open-handed Akbar showered lands, horses, and presents on the Mullá, who thus naïvely enough seeks in his annals to shield himself from the evil opinion which his base calumnies of his benefactor Faizí had laid him open to:—

"Should anyone, upon perusing this, observe that

Shaikh Faizí's regard and affection for me, which is widened by this letter, is but ill-requited by the harshness and severity with which I have spoken of him, especially after his death, when the precept of 'Speak not ill of the dead' should be strictly observed, I have only to reply that the observation is just; but under the circumstances, I inquire, what could I do? seeing that the truth of religion and the maintenance of one's faith are paramount to all other obligations, and that the maxim I never deviate from is, that my love and hatred should be subservient to God's cause. Although I was Shaikh Faizí's companion for forty years, nevertheless, after he apostatized from his religion, changed his manners, and entered on vain controversies, I became gradually estranged from him; and especially after what occurred at his death, I hold myself no longer his friend. When we are all summoned before the throne of God we shall receive sentence according to our deserts."

Here we leave sanctimonious and ungrateful 'Abdu-l-Kádir, and cannot refrain from quoting, as to the point, the fag-end of Thomas Moore's squib anent the late Leigh Hunt's somewhat similar treatment of the memory of Lord Byron, in which he warns "all lions well bred,"

Not to suffer small, mongrelly curs in their kitchen,
Who'll fawn on them living, and foul them when dead.

LVII.

THE COWARDLY MURDER OF THE WORTHY ABU-L-FAZL.

SAYS King Jahángír in his memoirs, "The Bundela Rájpút Rájá Narasingh Deo stood high in my favour. He was as brave, kind-hearted, and pure as any man of his age, and I made him a commander of 3,000, because at my instigation he had waylaid the Shaikh Abu-l-Fazl on his return from his government of the Dakhin.

"Abu-l-Fazl," continues Sháh Jahángír, "was not my friend, he inwardly nourished evil intentions towards me, and did not scruple to speak ill of me; so I entered into negotiations with Narasingh Deo, through whose country the Shaikh must needs pass on his homeward way from his southern government. God," (!) says this cold-blooded traitor and hypocrite, "rendered His aid to the success of the enterprize. The Rájá overwhelmed him and his followers, and he fell, his head being sent to me at Allahábád. My father's exasperation at this catastrophe gradually wore off, until at last I was allowed to visit him; his sorrow passed away and he received me with affection."

So, in spite of the assertion of the usually credible historian Farishta, that Abu-l-Fazl had been slain for the sake of booty by ordinary banditti, we have here distinct evidence under Jahángír's own hand, that he deliberately contrived the assassination of one of the most enlightened and able ministers who ever filled the Wazírat of Dehlí.

LVIII.

A FUGITIVE EMPEROR.

WHEN evil fortune overtook the brave and gentle Humáyun, he fled from his victorious opponent Shír Sháh from the field of Kanauj; and though he boldly strove to retrieve his past disasters, it was with such small avail, that he soon found himself a harassed fugitive on the way to Amarkot, beyond Thatta, in the parched-up land of Sindh.

Even when his horse showed signs of inability to proceed, and his faithful servant Tardí Bey offered him his own steed in its place, the Emperor refused the generous offer, and went on as he best could.

Followed and hard pressed by his relentless foe Máldeo, the Hindú Rájá of Ajmír, he was at length compelled to bestride a swift riding-camel for some time, until relieved by the loan of the horse of his foster-brother, Nadím Khán.

In the waterless wastes which they traversed, some became raving mad, whilst others died, but still Sháh

Humáyun pushed on; although "born in the purple," he shrank not before hardships which would have bewildered and prostrated weaker and less determined men.

As most of his historians remark, he had owed his downfall to his over-clemency to his adversaries. Sorry tribute this to Hindústání nature, and a stern warning to the present race of foreign rulers to have their hands of steel enveloped in velvet gloves.

Then, when the enemy came on in close pursuit, valiantly did the brave and fugitive monarch prepare to resist them and to preserve the wailing women and children who were in his train.

Sending his noble follower Amír Shaikh 'Alí to encounter them, that brave warrior smote down their leader, and they sought safety in flight.

Then those who had lost their way in the confusion came back to him, and kneeling in the midst of the wastes, the King and his men offered a humble thanksgiving to their Great Preserver.

Persecuted by unceasing thirst, when they at length reached a brook, men and camels so gorged themselves with water that they fell down and died.

At last the towers of the desert-fortress of Amarkot were seen, and in that town, so celebrated in after-days by its capture by our own Farangí chief Sir Charles Napier, the most renowned sovereign who ever reigned in Hind first saw the light. This was

Prince Akbar, the son of Baún Begum, who, though born under such sorry auspices, yet lived to raise the dynasty of his forbears to its highest.

As all were against the fallen monarch and sought to ingratiate themselves with the victorious Shír Sháh, Humáyun at last reluctantly fell back to Kandahár, where even his own brother 'Askarí Mírzá assailed him in fashion most unbrotherly in his deep distress.

The Persian Governor of Sístán greeted him, however, with the utmost cordiality, and furnished him and his faithful Queen with both money and attendants. At Hírát, the eldest son of the Sháh of Persia came forth to meet him, and as he went on towards Kazwín he was nobly entertained at every halt.

At Kazwín we, for the present, leave him.

LIX.

A ROYAL DRINKER.

"Bring up a child in the way he shall go, and when he is old he will not depart from it," so said Solomon the Wise, and the Emperor Jahángír of Hind differed not from him in opinion, for when his son Khurram came to be weighed, according to the Mughál custom, against jewels and gold, and even wheat, he told his son that as kings and princes drank wine, it behoved him to do so also. "To-day," said this accommodating parent, "is a festival, and I will drink wine with you, and you have leave to drink on feast-days, on New Year's Day, and at banquets, *in moderation*, for to drink to excess and enfeeble the intellect is eschewed by the wise, although much good may result from the imbibing of the juice of the grape in due season."

Jahángír says that until he reached the age of fourteen he never touched wine, except when it had been administered to him as a stimulant by his nurses when he was indisposed.

Once, he relates, his father mingled spirits with rose-water, and administered them to him as a cough-medicine; and how the Emperor of India gradually became a sot, we may recount in his own words:—

"In the days when my father was in the field against the Yúsufzaí Afgháns, and was encamped near Aták, I went one day to hunt, met with many mishaps, and, when I was utterly tired, listened to the advice of one of my servitors, who said that a cup of wine would refresh and do me good; then I swallowed a cup and a half of sweet yellow wine, and the result was pleasant, so that from that day I took to drinking, increasing my allowance day after day; and when plain grape-juice sufficed not, I began to drink ardent spirits, until at the end of nine years twenty cups of doubly-distilled spirit were my usual ration.

"Fourteen of these I imbibed by day, and the remaining six before I sought my couch.

"All my food at this time consisted of a single fowl and a little bread, and as I waxed wroth whenever my servitors dared to expostulate with me, I could, at last, scarcely hold my cup, after a more than usual debauch, for the shaking and trembling of my hand; so it went on till the cup had to be held to my mouth, and I sent for Doctor Humám, an old servant of my father, and asked him to cure me. Then that good man openly told me that if I did not discontinue my habits of drink, in six months there would be a new ruler of Hind."

So Jahángír attempted to reform, gradually diminishing the strength of his beverage by mixing wine with ardent spirits, and at the close of seven years six cups of eighteen miskáls and a quarter each were his *moderate* stint.

"For fifteen years," he continues, "I have now taken this quantity, I take it o' nights, except on Thursday, seeing that on that day I ascended the throne, and on Friday, the holiest day of the week, for I do not think it right to pass such nights in heedlessness, or to fail to thank the Almighty for his many blessings. On Thursdays and Sundays I abstain from meat, and pay especially honour to those days, because on the first I became Emperor, and on the second my father came into the world."

At last this abstinent and great Mughál took a fancy to opium, a weakness almost quite as general in Hindústán to this day, as it is in the Celestial Empire of China, and being then in his forty-sixth year he gravely and graciously informs posterity that he daily administered to himself fourteeen surkhs of opium (each surkh being equivalent to $1\frac{5}{16}$ of a grain Troy).

Yet even these excesses did not hinder him from becoming an old man, which proves that Sháh Jahángír had a tolerably good constitution.

LX.

NÚR-JAHÁN BEGUM.

WHEN Khwájá A'yás, who came of an old and noble but decayed family in Western Tartary, found that he was unable to support his young and loving wife, he resolved to seek fortune in that goal of all Tartar adventurers, the land of Hind. Placing his spouse on a miserable steed, he trudged manfully on his way, until his few coins had been expended, and the two forlorn wanderers found themselves in the midst of desolate wastes, with no succour near and at the mercy of the inclement weather and inhospitable climate. Three days passed without food, and, as if to complete their misery, the poor woman was seized with the pangs of childbirth, and showered reproaches on her husband for his rash expedition in search of uncertain benefits through assured hardships. At last a little girl made her appearance, and as no travellers appeared to aid them in their dire extremity and wild beasts abounded in that wilderness, A'yás, in desperation, seated his wife on the horse, but found himself so weak as to be unable to proceed or to carry the new-born babe; then began a grievious struggle between parental feeling and necessity, and at last the latter had the upper hand, and the weeping parents limped on as best they could, leaving their offspring covered with leaves by the road-side under a solitary tree. But maternal love was too powerful, and scarcely had the wretched couple progressed a mile when the wife entreated her husband to bring her little daughter back to her. On his return to the tree, A'yás was horrified by beholding a large black snake coiled round his infant child. His shouts terrified the reptile, who retreated into a hollow of a tree, and but for the timely arrival of the father the "Light of the World" would have been quenched. Brought back in safety to her mother, Providence sent some travellers to the rescue, who relieved their wants for the nonce, and slowly and wearily they plodded on until they reached the great city of Lahore, where Akbar the Sultán at that time kept his Court. Now, it so happened that one of the Emperor's most favoured lords, the Amír A'saf Khán, a distant relation of A'yás, was at that time in attendance on the monarch, and through his kindness the two wayfarers at last found themselves in a safe and comfortable asylum after all their hardships.

From at first being Private Secretary to A'saf Khán, A'yás became chief of a thousand horse, when his talents and zeal had commended him to the notice of an Emperor who possessed a rare discernment in the choice of his servitors. Promotion came rapidly on the fortunate Tartar, until the former wanderer in the desert found himself Master of the Imperial Household and High Treasurer of the Empire.

The "desert-born" girl had been named "Mihru-n-Nissá," or the "Sun amongst Women," a name which, by her great beauty, her skill in music, dancing, and in poetical composition, she well deserved. With a high and haughty spirit, she was the foremost amongst the liveliest and wittiest of her sex, and when brought veiled before the Prince Salím, afterwards Jahángír, who was her father's guest, the ill-concealed beauties of her form and the charm of her song so enraptured the heir to the throne, that he utterly lost his self-possession. Suddenly, and as if by accident, the ambitious coquette let fall her veil, and the fleeting glance which she then bestowed on the enamoured Salím so overcame him that he remained in silent thought during the rest of the evening. When the prince on the morrow solicited his father, Sultán

Akbar, to allow him marry the lady of his love, the Sultán's strong ideas of honour led him to refuse most sternly to interfere, inasmuch as "the Sun amongst Women" had already been formally betrothed by her father to the renowned Turkí noble Shír Afkan. The prince had to give way; the marriage was duly celebrated, but the husband was ever after pursued unceasingly by the vengeance of his princely and jealous rival, who caused him to be so slighted at Court, that he at length withdrew in disgust to Bengal, where he obtained the Government of Bardhwán. When the great Akbar was no more and Jahángír was "monarch of all he surveyed," he strove to persuade Shír Afkan to come to Court; but that stalwart and inflexible warrior guessed his object, and was in no mood to allow his conjugal honour to be trodden in the mire even by a king. He derived his "sobriquet" from his having slain a tiger single-handed; he had been one of Akbar's best soldiers, and his daring and intrepidity were the theme of every tongue. Still, he had no choice but to obey the Imperial command, and when honours without limit were poured on him by his insidious sovereign he began to believe that time and sensual indulgence elsewhere had effaced the first impressions created by his wife on the mind of Prince Salím; but here he was woefully mistaken, and many vile attempts were made to deprive him surreptitiously of life, which were warded off by his gigantic strength and wonderful courage. At length he left the capital and made his way back to Tánda in Bengal, where Kutb was governor; and as this mean satellite was well aware of what was the common talk of the courtiers, he secretly resolved to raise himself in the favour of his master by removing the obstacle which stood between him and his desires. When Shír learned that forty bravoes had been hired by Kutb to put him out of the world, he took no precautions, but, trusting solely to his own skill, strength, and valour, remained without armed attendants in his dwelling. An old darwán, or porter, alone stood sentry, and during his temporary absence the miscreants entered and concealed themselves in the house. Unaware that the wolves were shut up in the fold, Shír and his family bolted the doors and then went to bed, and when the assassins sneaked into his room he started from his couch, and after cutting many of them down, put the others to ignoble flight. Finally, the observed of all observers, he retired to his old place of sojourn at Bardwán, and when the zealous Kutb followed him up in order to carry out the base decrees of Jahángír, he and several nobles fell by the hands of the gallant "Tiger Slayer," who at last perished by the darts and bullets of enemies who were too dastardly to come to close quarters with so deadly and determined a swordsman. When the deed of darkness had been consummated the lady was packed off to Dehlí, but did not at first meet with the reception for which her ambition yearned. Jahángír caused her to be placed in one of the meanest of the apartments reserved for women, and only allowed her about two shillings a day for her own support and that of some female slaves. This unaccountable behaviour sorely distressed the haughty woman, who well knew that the splendour of her beauty would soon overpower the Emperor could he be prevailed on to see her. Luckily, she had a powerful ally at Court in the shape of the Emperor's own mother, who was a sincere advocate of her cause. For a long time the monarch kept aloof from Mihru-n-Nissá in spite of the pleadings of his own maternal parent, until she shamed him by executing and sending out for public sale articles of luxury of her own invention and manufacture, the beauty and delicacy of which far surpassed the productions of others, and became matter of public gossip. Four years did she vegetate thus without ever catching a glimpse of the moody Emperor; but at last the curiosity engendered by the marvellous reports of her mode of eking out the scanty and mean support she received from him, proved too great to be restrained, and without warning he suddenly entered her apartments, which were so elegantly, richly, and tastefully furnished that he was overcome with wonderment. There lay the enchantress, lightly clad in simple white muslin, while her slaves, attired in rich brocades, were seated around her, needle in hand. Rising in surprise, she stood before Jahángír, and, after gracefully saluting him, kept her eyes fixed on the ground. Enraptured by her beauty, Sháh Jahán could no longer control his feelings and took her at once into his arms. The next day their public nuptials were celebrated with every magnificence, and her name was changed to Núr Mahal or Núr Jahán, for by both is she known.

From that day to the end of Jahángír's reign she was undisputed mistress not only of the monarch, but of the Mughál Empire, and all her family partook of her increase of fortune. Worthiest of all of these was the ex-wanderer in the wilds, her father Khwájá A'yás, who doubtless often thanked his stars that he returned in time to rescue his forsaken child from the jaws of the black snake, and whose name is yet revered in the land of Hind as a great and virtuous minister.

Under his "wazírat," and whilst his enamoured son-in-law forgot the cares of State in the arms of the "Light of the World," foreign conquest was less thought of than home-improvement; agriculture was cherished, provinces wasted by former misrule and war were repeopled and brought once more into cultivation; property and industry were well safe-guarded, and arts were revived. Absence of oppression extinguished rebellion; and as idleness was not countenanced, robberies became things of the past.

In the administration of justice, both Musulmán and Hindú were on an equal footing.

Whilst her father kept the Empire in order, Núr Jahán reigned supreme within the precincts of the palace over her besotted and infatuated lord and master, whose dignity she contrived to preserve, notwithstanding his incurable tendency to debauchery, sometimes of the lowest kind.

When Prince Khuram (afterwards Sháh Jahán) had cleverly put down the rebellious Ráná of Audípúr, he was long supported by the influence of the Empress whose niece he had espoused, and at this period of the history of the reign, Sir Thomas Roe, Ambassador of King James the First, of Gunpowder Plot memory, was received at Ajmír by Sháh Jahángír. Roe did not think much of the Upper Ten Thousand of the time in Hindústán (A.D. 1615), for he describes them as venal and corrupt; but he says that Jahángír had images of Jesus Christ and the Virgin Mary attached to his rosary or tasbíh. Il Musannif now leaves other events of the reign of Jahángír aside, and goes back to the "Light of the World."

At last she lost her father the good 'Itimádu-d-Daulah, and grand was the monument she erected to his memory in Akbarábád.

The silent and bigoted hypocrite Sháh Jahán's designs had not escaped her, and she communicated her suspicions to her husband, but not before the future

Emperor of Hind had removed his brother Khusrú from the scene by the hands of hired murderers and then pretended to be ignorant of the crime.

But when his wiles were of no effect he took refuge from the wrath of his incensed father in open rebellion. In the year 1031 of "the Departure" he assumed the ensigns of royalty and marched towards Dehlí; he was then proclaimed a rebel, and as the far-seeing Sultán had already mustered forces against his rebellious son, after a great fight in the midst of a dust-storm, Jahángír had the best of the day, and Sháh Jahán fled to the hills of Míwát, and continued obstinate in his unfilial treason. After many reverses he was routed in Bengal by Muhabbat Khán, his father's best officer, and hunted like a wild beast from place to place, till at last his repentant letters prevailed on his too easy father to overlook his offences.

Núr Jahán's constant interferences had incensed Muhabbat Khán, who had been treated with gross indignity in the person of a near relative at the instigation of the Empress. Followed by his Rájpúts, that chief burst suddenly into the Emperor's tent and seized his person, and whilst the nominal authority of Jahángír was outwardly maintained, Muhabbat was the Mayor of the Palace and real master of the situation as he was of his sovereign's body. Hearing of these occurrences, Núr Jahán escaped to her brother A'saf, the Wazír, who marched instantly to the Sultán's rescue.

Fighting at a disadvantage at the fords of Jailam, many of the men of A'saf Jáh were drowned in the rapid river or cut down by the men of Muhabbat on the slippery opposite bank. Foremost in the fight was the heroine Núr Jahán, who plunged on her elephant into the stream, whilst her little daughter seated on her knee in the haudah was wounded by an arrow, three of her mahâwats were killed, and thrice her elephant was wounded in the trunk. All this time, bow in hand, she emptied four quivers of arrows at the men of Muhabbat Khán. "Truly, an Amazon of Hind was Núr Jahán," says Il Musannif.

At last she was turned away most unwillingly from the fight by her Master of the Household; and as the victory remained with Muhabbat Khán, she fled to Lahore, where she was persuaded by letters from her husband, written at the dictation of Muhabbat Khán, to come and join him. This she did, and was then placed under surveillance and even condemned to death as a persistent disturber of the peace of the realm. The Emperor, who had signed her death-warrant, had to beg her life from Muhabbat, and she was released. Muhabbat was warned by his friends that the Sultána would never forget her condemnation, and when the Imperial army, nominally directed by Jahángír, but in reality controlled by Muhabbat, reached Kábul, the Emperor was a mere puppet in the hands of his able minister. Fond of private ease, the Emperor found himself more secure with the resolute and far-seeing Muhabbat Khán as his mouth-piece than he had ever been before; but the galled spirit of the "Light of the World" was not so placable, and with womanly wile and treachery she hatched schemes for the destruction of her too-forgiving foe, who, not trusting anybody but his tried and faithful Rájpúts, invariably camped outside the city of Kábul. The citizens of that town, at the instigation of the Empress, rose in arms against him, and he narrowly escaped from their hands. To revenge this conduct of the ancestrally perfidious and murderous Kábulís, he established such a strict blockade of the faithless city that they were fain to sue for mercy. History repeats itself, they say, and the story of poor Louis Cavagnari is only one amongst the many samples of the treachery of a race whom nothing but the sword or the rope will compel into even the semblance of loyalty or honesty.

Sick of Kábul and its miscreant inhabitants, he signified to the Emperor on the morrow that he must be ready to march back to Lahore; but, on the way, being moved by no mean ambition and having sought from the first nought but the well-being of the empire, he returned to Jahángír all his suspended authority, and even dismissed many of his trusty Rájpúts. Now was the time for the revenge of the unscrupulous and vindictive Queen, who, however, at first was checked by her husband, who would listen to no suggestion, however insidiously conveyed, of harm to one whom he had found to be a good man and true.

Private assassination of her enemy was then plotted, but the Emperor heard of his wife's plans and warned Muhabbat when they were on the banks of the Jailam. He escaped alone, and all his property was confiscated by Núr Jahán, who lost no time in setting a price on his head. Away went the fallen chief to his relative A'saf, who then lay in camp at Karnál, and the two determined that they would do their best to raise the Prince Sháh Jahán to the masnad. When this intelligence reached Jahángír he restored Muhabbat to all his honours and reversed his outlawry, but that commander would not trust himself to the ill-faith of the wicked woman who had so often schemed his destruction, and whilst he was still balancing in his mind, news came of the death of Sultán Jahángír at the town of Muttí, between Kashmír and Lahore, in the year of our Lord 1627, and on the ninth day of the month of November, in the fifty-eighth year of his age, and after a reign of over twenty-two years.

Then A'saf Khán marched into the Panjáb as the supporter of Sháh Jahán, and defeated and blinded Prince Shahryár, who had been appointed successor by Jahángír at the instigation of Núr Jahán, and advised Muhabbat, who was at that time at Golconda with the future monarch, of what had passed. Then, to make a long story short, Sháh Jahán initiated his reign by the murder of his brother and other relatives who might possibly in the future have interfered with his sovereignty, only he and his own children remaining of the posterity of Bábar the Conqueror of Hind.

And now Il Musannif comes to the close of the strange and romantic history of Núr Jahán Begum, who died peaceably in Lahore after having long led the life of a recluse and been handsomely treated by Sháh Jahán. Her tomb was raised in the same city after her decease in A.D. 1646, by the side of the mausoleum of Jahángír. So at last this turbulent, intriguing, and beautiful woman was finally at rest; and would that all her sex were as harmless as she now is, says ungallant Il Musannif.

LXI.

THE UNHAPPY POSSESSOR OF A DIAMOND-STREAM.

Now the Rájpút Zamíndár, Durjan Sál, who dwelt as Kokrah in the province of Bihár, would have been a happy man had not a stream traversed his estate, with the sand and pebbles of which diamonds were intermingled.

When the water of this brook was low in the hot season the practised diamond-searchers were guided to the precious nodes by small gnats, by them called chíkás; wherever this buzzing insect was found to prevail dams of stone were erected, and delving with spade and pick began vigorously. Small and large diamonds frequently rewarded their toils, and some of the latter brought no less than a lac of rupees to their finders.

The greedy Muhammadan who governed the province had frequently attempted to master this district; but Durjan Sál, from the depths of his jungles and morasses, long kept them away, and defied all the efforts of the would-be marauder Zafar Khán.

When, however, the latter chief had been displaced by Ibráhím Khán, the tidings of this tempting field of gain had already reached the Imperial ears of Sultán Jahángír at Dehlí.

Coveting so wealthy a possession, this true descendant of Mughál banditti caused a sudden raid to be made into the territory of Kokrah, and Durjan Sál, being unprepared for resistance, fell with all his family into the hands of the grasping invader. Great was the capture of diamonds and elephants, and the grateful Emperor not only increased the personal salary of Ibráhím Khán to 4,000 tankás, but gave him the title of "Victory in War" and the command of 4,000 horse.

What became of poor Durjan Sál the Unlucky, the Imperial scribe does not relate, but he gloats over the proceeds of this act of brigandage, and tells us that "diamonds of the value of 50,000 rupees had been already discovered, and that he hopes that a continuance of the search may be rewarded by further success, and that more excellent diamonds may find their way to the repository of the Crown jewels."

Little did the haughty Jahángír deem, when he wrote this, that most of these and still more costly gems were foredoomed to fall to the share of that still greater brigand, Sháh Nádír, in after days.

LXII.

A VALIANT ROBBER.

In the eleventh year of the reign of Jahángír (A.D. 1616), when James the First of England and Sixth of Scotland was ruler of the British Isles, the Hindú thieves carried on their nefarious profession with the utmost audacity and success within the very precincts of the Imperial city of Dehlí, and even presumed to loot the treasury of the Kotwálí or Chief Office of the Police.

Then when severe search had been made to discover these daring ruffians, seven fell into the hands of the authorities, amongst whom was a certain Narnal, their chief.

Some were tortured to death or cut into minute

pieces, but the chief chastisement was reserved for their ringleader, who was doomed to be crushed beneath the feet of an elephant.

Earnestly he besought the Emperor to allow him to fight the gigantic beast for his life; and the monarch was moved, probably by the expectation of beholding an entirely new diversion, to consent to the malefactor's petition.

With a dagger only, the bold culprit faced the elephant; though many times cast to the earth, he as often recovered his feet, and so mutilated the trunk of his opponent with his weapon, that the beast shrieked loudly, after the manner of his kind, and declined to continue the contest.

Such courage met with due reward from the despot, and the brave criminal was pardoned and cared for, until, pining once more for his former wild mode of life, he abandoned the purlieus of the Court and sought refuge in the jungle.

When this ungrateful proceeding reached the ears of Jahángír, his wrath was kindled, and an edict went forth to the jágírdárs of the surrounding districts to use every effort to recapture Narnal under pain of the Imperial displeasure.

So Narnal was at last taken and duly hanged.

LXIII.

SULTÁN JAHÁNGÍR DESCRIBES A TURKEY.

Amongst other rarities which the Sultán received from the Portuguese of Goa, was what to him was a very remarkable specimen of ornithology, but which is now common enough in the land of Hind, where it is known as the Pírú; in his memoirs he thus depicts it: "One of the birds resembled a peahen, but was a little larger in size, though smaller than a peacock. When he was desirous of pairing, he used to spread his tail and feathers, and danced about like a peacock. His beak and feet resembled those of a barn-door fowl, his head, neck, and throat changed their colour every minute; but when anxious to pair he became a perfect red, and seemed to be a beautiful piece of coral. After some time he was as white as coral, and sometimes became as blue as a turquoise, and, in short, turned all colours like a chameleon. The piece of flesh on his head was like the crest of a cock; but the strangest part of it was that this piece of flesh whenever he wished to pair hung down a span long, like the trunk of an elephant, and when again restored to its position it was erected over his head like the horn of a rhinoceros. The part round his eyes remained constantly of a blue colour, and never changed, which was not the case with his wings, which were always changing their colour."

The same Emperor, whilst marching through the Panjáb on his way to Kábul, A.D. 1603, had the misfortune to lose by death his favourite antelope Ráj, who had been the best fighter in Jahángír's possession, and a skilled decoy for the wild ones of his species. Over this animal's remains a minaret-tomb was erected, and the animal's figure carved in stone. "Out of regard for this animal," says the monarch, "I ordered that no man should hunt antelopes in that hunting-ground, and that their flesh should be considered as unlawful as that of a cow to the infidel Hindús, and as that of the hog to the Musulmáns."

Truly, that antelope was a benefactor to his kind.

LXIV.

EUROPEAN ACCOUNTS OF JAHÁNGÍR.

CATROW says "the religion of the Christians was agreeable to him, chiefly on account of the license which it affords for the use of wine and the flesh of all kinds of animals." This was the only view he took of it. That spirit of patience, humility, charity, and temperance, which is the soul of Christianity, was never a subject on which he reflected. With prepossessions founded on such impure motives did he declare himself openly in favour of the Christians, and violate, without scruple, the rule of Muhammad. He drank wine in the face of his own Court.

Sir Thomas Roe writes, "Four or five cases of red wine should be sent as presents to the King and Prince, as never were men more enamoured of that drink as these two, and which they would more highly esteem than all the jewels in Cheapside."

Catrow again says, "It was more particularly during the night that the King gave himself up to intoxication, in the society of his friends. All the Franks in Agra—that is, all Europeans of whatsoever nation—were allowed free access to the palace. He continued drinking in this company till the return of day, and he abandoned himself especially to these debaucheries at a season which the Muhammadans observe as a fast (Ramazán) with the most scrupulous exactness. When some of his nation of rather rigid principles happened to be present at these meetings, he compelled them to violate their fast, threatening them, in case of disobedience, that they should be thrown to two lions, who were always kept chained beneath the windows of his apartments."

Hawkins says, "He goes into a private room, where for two years I was one of his attendants, and there he drinks five other cups of strong liquor; this done, he chews opium, and, being intoxicated, goes to sleep."

His wife, the famous Núr Jahán, had stinted him to nine goblets, but he disobeyed even her.

"Wine-houses, since the days of Akbar, had been tolerated in the capital; but this Emperor went in disguise to one of them, took a seat near a working-man who was drinking with great gaiety, and who, inspired by the wine, was disposed to indulge his vocal talents. Jahángír was delighted to find himself in such pleasant society. A familiarity was soon established between them, and the artisan was particularly charmed with the liberality of the new guest, who paid the entire score and made him drink deep."

LXV.

KHÁN JAHÁN LÚDÍ AND SHÁH JAHÁN.

The will of Jahángír, which had been made at the instigation of the Lady Núr Jahán in favour of his fourth son Shahryár, who was her favourite, was speedily set aside by the defeat and blinding of the latter; then Sháh Jahán, aided by his staunch allies A'saf and Muhabbat, marched towards the capital. He was, however, much snubbed by Khán Jahán Lúdí, who was commander in the Dakhin, and descended from a royal race. When Sháh Jahán was informed of the defeat of Shahryár by A'saf Khán, he caused his brother and two other near relations to be strangled, and then, in all the full-blown glory of Imperialism, pitched his tents in that garden near Agra which was known as "the Habitation of Light."

Either by the dagger or the cord, all the relatives of the new monarch were despatched to another world, and then the supporters of Sháh Jahán, A'saf and Muhabbat, were raised to the highest dignities in the State.

The beginning of this reign was steeped in the blood of his relations, but Sháh Jahán had firm possession of the vast empire of his father, and one of his first steps was to repay Khán Jahán Lúdí for the disrespect he had shown him when he was as yet but an aspirant for the throne. For a time an invasion of the Usbaks, who had beleaguered Kábul, delayed the execution of his design, but as soon as that was quelled, along with some troubles in Bundhelkand, he had to deal with the revolt of Khán Jahán, who, after having apparently submitted, had drawn his sword to protect himself and his son from the assassination which the vindictive and treacherous monarch had planned during a public reception in the Palace at Agra. Escaping thence to his own dwelling, and finding himself encompassed by his mortal foes, he determined either to cut his way through them or die in the attempt.

But to leave his women to be dishonoured was intolerable, and as he hesitated in his desperation which course to pursue in such a terrible strait, his female relations retired from his presence and deliberately committed suicide. Hearing their dying groans, he rushed into the darkened apartment whence the cries proceeded, and when a light was brought the whole floor of the room was seen to be flooded with the blood of these unfortunates.

Burying the dead in the garden, and allowing himself some short time for silent grief, he gathered his retainers together to the sound of martial music, and rushing like a whirlwind through the dismayed troops of Sháh Jahán, issued from Agra and made for Málwa. Pursued by the Imperialists, and stopped by the flooded and rapid Chambal, he defended a pass, of which with military genius he possessed himself, like a hero; none of his followers blenched before the superior numbers of the assailants, and his valiant son 'Asmat died nobly in protecting his father's retreat across the river, into which he had plunged on horseback.

Unable to avenge brave 'Asmat, whose men had perished with him to the last, after having fearfully mauled their opponents, Khán Jahán continued his flight with the Imperialists at his heels. Driven from his own province of Málwa before he could get his friends together, he fought his way like a lion at bay to the country of the Bundelas, until the wearied troops of the Emperor abandoned the pursuit.

Received in most friendly wise by his warm friend the Nizám at Dalautábád, Sháh Jahán became alarmed, and resolved to head an army in person wherewith to crush so talented and uncompromising a foe, and in the month of February A.D. 1631, he went forward with a force of 300,000 men, of whom 100,000 were horsemen. Although the Musulmán Princes of Southern and Mid-India kept aloof from the Mughál Sovereign, their fears for their own well-being kept them from siding heartily with the Lúdí chief, and the Emperor's deputies were generally successful.

Still Khán Jahán remained a thorn in the Imperial side; he harassed the Mughál troops unceasingly, and things long remained in suspense, in spite of the small means at his command, until the Sultán of the Mughals determined to send his minister A'saf into the field. That general routed the Lúdí and his allies, and the former escaped after many vicissitudes to Díbálpúr. Thence he wandered, a hunted fugitive, until his retinue was reduced near Kalijar to about thirty good men and true, and with these, who preferred rather to die with than to desert their leader, he charged the troops of his pursuer Muzaffar, and fell dead by a musket-shot with all his faithful companions around him.

Thus died this valorous and able chieftain, whose head was placed on high over the gates of Burhánpúr, much as the heads of the Scottish nobles of '45 were stuck over Temple Bar in 1746 by that high-minded Hanoverian monarch Georgius Secundus; and all his slayers received high rank and great "largesse," as others did in

Scotland during the last century for similar actions. "God bless the Duke of Argyll," says Il Musannif.

LXVI.

HOW SHÁH JAHÁN'S UNFILIAL TRANSGRESSIONS CAME HOME TO HIM.

NEWS reached the astute Prince Aurangzíb in the south that his father the Sultán was perilously ill, and that his brother Dárá Shikoh was taking every precaution to secure his own accession to the "masnad" in the event of the death of Sháh Jahán. Joining with his brother Murád, he prepared for war, and after gaining the great Mír Jumlah over to his views, he set forth from the city of Aurangábád on the 16th day of February in the year of our Lord 1658, and after a desperate and dubious struggle with the Mahárájá Jaswant Singh, entered Ujjain in triumph.

Consternation reigned in the Court of Dehlí on the receipt of these tidings, and Dárá's irresolution led to mournful results. Sent to encounter his brothers, he entrenched himself strongly on the line of the Chambal, where, as Aurangzíb and his dashing brother Murád found his position impregnable, they very cleverly left their camp standing in order to delude the enemy, and when Dárá became aware of their manœuvres they were already between him and the capital. He had been thoroughly out-generalled, but by a hasty march he again posted himself between them and Agra, and on the 4th of June of the same year he confronted them in open battle. Valiantly did all these sons of Sháh Jahán comport themselves, but victory smiled on Murád and Aurangzíb, and Dárá was compelled to unwilling flight.

This crowning victory was fought some sixteen miles from Agra, and the conquerors, astounded at their unexpected good fortune, abstained from pursuit, and stayed awhile in order to reinvigorate their exhausted troops. Much manhood showed the aged and infirm Emperor when he heard of this crushing defeat, but Dárá made haste to Dehlí, quoting some "ghazls" of Háfiz to cheer him and his disheartened followers during his flight. The treasure on which he chiefly depended for the raising of fresh levies was looted by Ját Hindú robbers, and yet he contrived to get together a respectable force in a brief space of time.

His son, the warlike and able Sulaimán, whose talents and resolution were likely to prove the chief obstacles to the ambition of Aurangzíb, found himself deserted by his troops near Allahábád, and although Murád and Aurangzíb pitched their tents near the defenceless capital on the 9th of June, the latter affected moderation because his schemes were not yet ripe for execution, and the former was prostrate from the severe wounds he had received in the late battle.

Sháh Jahán was beloved by the people, although his rebellious offspring were at the gates of the citadel, and when he caused those gates to be shut Aurangzíb resolved to make guile the substitute for more open and violent measures.

At this time, whilst he professed to be averse to the pretensions of Dárá, he feigned to uphold the claims of his brother Murád, who was no hypocrite, and could neither hide his hatred nor his love. Murád roughly snubbed his sister, Jahán-A'rá, who had been sent to the brothers by Sháh Jahán in order to bring about an understanding, and the offended princess was then persuaded by Machiavellian Aurangzíb to espouse his views to the detriment of Murád. After drawing from her sisterly trustfulness everything that could be turned against Dárá Shikoh, and making sickening protestations of piety and filial affection, he sent her back, thoroughly duped, with a message of peace and love to the ancient King, who then and there reversed his decision, and consented to look on Aurangzíb as a paragon of filial duty, and on Murád as a haughty and faithless upstart.

Still mindful of his own treachery to his father Jahángír, who had steadfastly characterised himself as *the wretch* in his "Memoirs," he determined to make sure of Aurangzíb by seizing his person so soon as he should enter the citadel. An intercepted letter betrayed his intentions to Aurangzíb, but that wide-awake prince kept his own counsel, and took measures according to the information he had received, and, in lieu of appearing in person to prostrate himself at the feet of his father and Sovereign, sent his son Muhammad into the citadel as his substitute, on the 15th of June 1658. Muhammad was accompanied by a guard, which were admitted by the King. This party was judiciously posted in the most commanding positions of the fortress, and, on the other hand, Sháh Jahán had placed a body of armed retainers within the precincts of the seraglio. Muhammad discovered this, and warned his grandfather that Aurangzíb would never trust himself within the gates unless these men were ordered out of the place. Sháh Jahán appears to have thought that the robust and armed Tartár women and the eunuchs of his harem would prove sufficent for his purpose. The arrival of Aurangzíb was then expected with intense anxiety by both his father and his son, but although the crafty deceiver mounted his horse and rode forward, he caused farther delay by halting his cavalcade for the purpose of offering up prayers at the tomb of his great ancestor Akbar. Vain was the rage of Sháh Jahán, who saw himself outwitted by his grandson, who was, *de facto,* master of the citadel and of his Imperial person. Touching were his appeals to Muhammad, who was greatly moved, but finding all his entreaties wasted, he at last sent the keys of the fortress to Aurangzíb, whose natural hypocrisy and deeply designing nature still kept him aloof from a personal interview. Said he in a letter, "Dárá is alone blameworthy, the misfortunes of the Emperor are all his work, and when I have disabled him from doing further mischief I will myself come and open the gates of the fortress in which my parent can in the meanwhile pass his time in that serene tranquillity which befits his advanced years."

Aurangzíb then proceeded to humbug Murád, whom he acknowledged as his lord and master, and with mock humility he even stated his intention of passing the remainder of his days in the Holy Places of Arabia, "where he might be shielded from the turmoils and evil devices of the world." Murád swallowed all this for a time, but, when undeceived as to his brother, secretly determined to get rid of Aurangzíb at a dinner party at Mathurá. But the latter shammed sick, and, absenting himself from the festal board, inveigled his brother into his own quarter of the camp to an entertainment of which wine and women were the prominent features. Once there and thoroughly intoxicated, Murád was seized after a desperate resistance, and sent off under a strong guard to Agra.

In the meantime Dárá Shikoh had levied strength in "the country of the Five Rivers," and Aurangzíb, after assuming the Imperial authority, marched in person against him, and Dárá's son Sulaimán was as unfortunate as his father. Although posted strongly along the Biyás river, Dárá's hesitation allowed the men of Aurangzíb to out-manœuvre him, and his troops dropped away by hundreds before the pursuit of Khán-i-Jahán. Mír Jumlah now made friends with the rising sun, and unlucky Dárá continued his flight *viá* Multán, and through Bhakkar to the mountain-ranges beyond the Indus.

Muhabbat, who ruled in Kábul, and had always entertained an intense aversion for the false and treacherous Aurangzíb, now stood up in arms, and the state of things at Agra called earnestly for the presence of the new Emperor. Many looked on his treatment of his father as more than ordinarily vile, and the old man, although in honourable confinement, had still many well-wishers and friends left to him; but Aurangzíb's known ability ranged most of the nobles on his side, and when his brother Shujá entered the field as his competitor, and the rival forces met in the district of Allahábád, January 13th, 1659, after one of the fiercest contests ever known in India, the field remained to Aurangzíb, whose baggage was nevertheless plundered by the retreating Rájpúts of the Mahárájá Jaswant Singh, who carried off their booty in safety.

Away rode the fugitive Shujá to Patna, but still firm and self-reliant, and knowing that he would find many supporters in that province of Bengal which he had ruled so justly and so well.

After a most sanctimonious speech to cloak his nefarious designs, and a politic distribution of rewards and punishments to those who had distinguished or misbehaved themselves during the late battle, he sent Mír Jumlah and his son Muhammad in pursuit of the fugitive Shujá, and then returned to the capital, where his canting letter to his father was returned to him unopened, with these words: "If my son means to insult me, to know it would but add to my misfortunes; if he treats me with affection and respect, why does he let me languish within these walls?"

When Dárá had crossed the Indus he made his way through burning deserts, tangled jungles, and mountain-paths to Ahmadábád in Gujárát, where Sháh-Nawáz, the father-in-law of both Aurangzíb and Murád, still ruled. Sháh-Nawáz was at first inclined to favour the cause of Aurangzíb, but the entreaties of the wife of Murád in behalf of Dárá caused such a revulsion of feeling, that he became a strong partisan of the fugitive prince, who, had he listened to the advice of the Rájpút Mahárájá Jaswant Singh, and not procrastinated, might have overthrown the still ill-cemented fabric of the new Empire.

But Aurangzíb's policy prevented Jaswant Singh from becoming an active foe, and Dárá, with his European engineers, entrenched himself on the main road from Ajmír to Dehlí in a commanding position. Seeing that it would be folly to assail his impregnable brother, the astute usurper determined to draw him forth, and by means of spurious letters he effectually succeeded in this design owing to the impetuous character of a brother who could brook neither slight nor denial. His men slipped round into the entrenchments which the imprudent Dárá had left open to them, and a general consternation pervaded the army of Dárá Shikoh, who, seeing himself overcome, rode off to Gujarát, after having had his own baggage plundered by some subsidiary Maráthás, who thought it a holy action to despoil a Muhammadan prince, and whose sordid cupidity had no reverence even for a ruined and forsaken man. With a few miserable tents which still remained to hide his harem from the gaze of the profane, a couple of elephants, and a scanty following, this Prince of Misfortune once more found the desolate and burning tract which divides Gujarát from the Valley of the Indus. But when he reached Sindh, although his immediate wants were relieved, no succour of men or arms would the Jám vouchsafe him. On he wandered through frightful hardships, losing the greater part of his retinue on the way, and daily he had to inter some faithful friend or follower. When in sight of Thatta, he and his were so utterly exhausted that he was obliged to present himself in person at the next village in search of relief.

There was one chief, Jihon Khán by name, who had twice owed his life to the intercession of the hunted

Dárá, and much did he simulate hospitality and respect to the unhappy prince. In his fortalice the brave wife Sultána Nádirah, who had clung to her lord devotedly throughout all his perilous wanderings, succumbed.

"I was not bereft of friendship," said the mourning Dárá, "as long as my well-loved Nádirah lived, but her eyes are now closed to the misfortunes which are in store for her husband and her children."

Believing that even the traitor Aurangzíb would not be wanting in respect to the remains of his deceased consort, Dárá sent them under escort to Lahore, and then took leave of his treacherous entertainer, who immediately followed with a superior force and brought him in bonds to Khán Jahán, who could not refrain from tears when he beheld the manly demeanour of the fallen son of Sháh Jahán.

When fraternal Aurangzíb held his own father's son in his clutches, he ignominiously paraded him, in a beggar's dress and on a sorry elephant, through the streets of Dehlí, but the great crowds that had assembled to witness this shameful spectacle so sympathized with the wretched captive that they unanimously burst into tears and reviled Aurangzíb. He was then placed in durance vile at Khizrábád, outside Dehlí, and confined in a miserable den, together with his son, with the dread of assassination perpetually before his eyes.

The traitor Jihon, who had come to receive the reward of his perfidy, was waylaid and put to death by the indignant country-people, and as a general insurrection in favour of the imprisoned prince seemed imminent, away went Názir and Saif, two savage Afgháns, to do the deed of blood, the perpetration of which is thus related by the native annalist:

"On the 11th of September, about midnight, the unfortunate prince was startled from his sleep by the approach of armed men; scarcely had he roused his son, when the assassins forced the door, and Dárá, whose only weapon was a common pen-knife, stood at bay with his son in a corner. The murderers ordered the removal of the lad, but he still clung round his father's knees. Falling on the youth's neck, Dárá told him to live to avenge him, and the bravoes then proceeded to strangle him, but deeming this an ignominious death, he, with one vigorous effort, stabbed one of the villains to the heart, and was then cut to pieces by the swords of the other reprobates."

Off went his head, which was borne to Aurangzíb, that that amiable relative might glut his eye-sight with the view of his murdered brother, whose headless corpse remained all night in the cell where the assassination had taken place, and in company with the bound and helpless orphan.

For many days the crowd were ignorant of this foul murder, but the wily hypocrite Aurangzíb won forgiveness from them by ostentatious liberality, and was then free to prosecute his campaign against Shujá in Bengal. Mír Jumlah's generalship overcame many difficulties and reverses, and Shujá was pursued with untiring energy through almost impervious woods and across deep valleys and plunging torrents, across the Brahmapútra, and to the frontiers of Arakan, which he reached with some forty followers. There the Rájá affected to believe him to be a conspirator against his life; affecting terror, the yellow-faced Magh summoned his council, and decided to put the fugitive to death. When this resolve was made known to Shujá, he was encamped with his handful of men on a plain between a precipice and a river. When the Arakanese troops were near at hand the descendant of Taimúr thus spoke to his few adherents: "The contest before us is unequal, but as we are situated, the issue may be fortunate; it is no fight for empire, or even for life, it is simply one for the honour of my race. Shujá can only die sword in hand, and as there is no price placed on your heads by Aurangzíb, as has been the case with mine, you have yet a fair chance of escape."

But his undaunted comrades refused to hearken to him, and deliberately took part by his side. Twice were the craven and overwhelming numbers of the infidels repulsed in hand-to-hand fight by the gallant few, until at last the adversaries resorted to their arrows, which, from a distance, smote down the greater portion of Shujá's friends. At last the idolators rolled down heavy stones from the rocks above, and one of them struck and stunned Shujá, who was then made a captive. On beholding this, his women cast themselves into the river, and the Arakanese, as soon as they had rowed their prisoner into the middle of the broad and rapid river, drew a large plug from the bottom of the canoe, and then escaped to another boat which was in waiting, whilst Shujá and his two remaining friends were engulfed in the waters. Perhaps the late M. Carrier, of Nantes and Noyades renown, had studied this little episode of Indian history, says Il Musannif.

In short, the whole family perished, and as space does not allow Il Musannif to deal further with the earlier villainies of Sultán Aurangzíb, that Louis Onze of Hindústán, who could lift one hand to invoke his God, and sign warrants for the murder of his nearest kinsmen with the other, he reverts to the latter end of Sháh Jahán, who heard of the destruction of his other and best-beloved sons, who chafed in his golden bonds like a tiger in his cage, and died at length, after having been swindled out of his remaining jewels by his mean son Aurangzíb.

Il Musannif has seen the glorious Táj at Agra, that crown of all tombs, in which repose until the "Youngest Day" the ashes of "the King of the Earth," and of his beloved Mumtáza Zamání.

LXVII.

SIVAJÍ, THE MARÁTHÁ.

When Sivají had gained the country between Chákur and the Nura, and had chosen an eyrie whence, like the wily tiger of his native jungles, he could spring on his unsuspecting prey, he occupied himself without cessation in gathering together and arming his Máwalís, whilst his Brahman emissaries spied out the land of Konkan. One of his first deeds of daring was to pounce with 300 horse upon a convoy of Government treasure, and to secure it in his mountain stronghold of Rájgarh; and, after having shown himself in his true character, he proceeded to greater extremes, and captured many important places, especially the precipitous mountain of Rairí, and the city of Kallian, where he appointed his own governor. All these proceedings caused great consternation at the Court of Dehlí, but the supine Sultán Muhammad 'Adil Sháh took no measures to repress the daring brigand of Maháráshtra, except by enticing Sháhjí, the father of Sivají, who governed the province of the Karnátik, to his Court, and detaining him as a hostage. Father and son were allowed to correspond, and the former, to show his own loyalty to the King, strongly proposed that Sivají should be brought to obedience by force of arms; the monarch, however, refused to credit his being aught but an accomplice in the rebellion of his offspring, and cruelly thrust the old man into a deep dungeon, the entrance to which was almost entirely built-up, with the intimidation that if within a certain time his son did not submit, the small opening would be closed up altogether. Much moved was Sivají when these tidings of his parent's peril came to his ears, and he would fain have wrought his deliverance by submission had not his resolute wife impressed on him that he had a far better chance of attaining his object by increasing and maintaining his power than by placing any confidence in so notoriously unscrupulous and treacherous a government as that of Bíjápúr.

Acquiring, by wily diplomacy, the good will of the Emperor Sháh Jahán, through the intercession of that sovereign Sivají obtained his father's liberation from the dungeon, but not permission to leave the city of Bíjápúr, where he was held under surveillance during yet another four years. It is pleasant to see such filial affection displayed by one whose red hand was against everyone, and had everyone's hand against him. During this period he committed but few aggressions for fear of endangering the safety of Sháhjí, who was at last allowed to proceed to his jágír in the Karnátak, where great disturbances had arisen. His departure left his son free from anxiety on his account, and he recommenced his raids and forays with still more vigour than before, and by the slaughter of the Hindú

Rájá of Jaulí and the capture of Rohíra, made still further progress towards the attainment of great power. The illness of Sháh Jahán saved him from the wrath of Aurangzíb, at that time Governor of the Dakhan, who patched up a peace with Bíjápúr, and then proceeded northward, where his energy, courage, duplicity, and cruelty soon proved the ruin of his brothers. He hesitated not to unseat his aged father Sháh Jahán, and to usurp the Imperial throne.

Then began a game of dissembling between two of the most thorough experts in that specially Eastern art in the land of Hind. Sivají promised fidelity, and vowed that the increase of his armed followers was due solely to the intense desire which filled him of being of service to the Emperor. Aurangzíb pardoned him and gave him leave to carry his arms into the Konkan, where his Peshwá, or leader Shámráj, was bitterly mauled by the rough-handed Abyssinian, or Sídí Janhar. In spite of its own enfeebled condition, the Court of Bíjápúr at last took heart of grace, to check the course of the undaunted marauder, and despatched for that purpose a well-appointed force of 12,000 men under Afzal Khán. Unable to face so powerful an antagonist, the Maráthá fell back on his citadel of Pratábgarh, and affected an intense desire to obtain forgiveness through the intercession of Afzal Khán, whom he lured into a private interview. The Muhammadan came unsuspectingly to the meeting, leaving his troops in the rear, whilst the Maráthás were secretly ambushed in every nook and corner around. Then, in order to fulfil the divine mission which he asserted he held from Bhuwaní, the "Goddess of Destruction," having performed his ablutions with much earnestness, he laid his head at his mother's feet, and begged her to bless him. Secretly protected by a coat of mail, which, together with a poniard he wore beneath his clothes, whilst in his left hand he held concealed that peculiarly shaped and terrible dagger, the "wagnuck," which this perfidious deed has rendered famous throughout Mahárásthtra, and infamous elsewhere, he approached the lightly-clad Muhammadan chief, and, pretending to enfold him in his arms, ripped him up with a treacherous stab; drawing out the wagnuck, he then plunged his other dagger into his foe's body. The Muhammadan died game, for, even when so mortally hurt, he made a desperate cut with his sword at his assassin, which was warded off by the hidden coat of mail.

The head of the murdered Afzal was in due Asiatic course cut off and carried into Pratábgarh, and the troops of Bíjápúr, surprised on all sides, and dismayed by the loss of their general, became the easy prey of the assassin. Sivají spared most of his captives, as, indeed, he generally did throughout his long and varied career, except in cases when rich men pretended to be penniless, then no cruelty was neglected which would draw their wealth from them. As one of his officers had taken a bribe to aid the escape of the son and family of the late Afzal, Sivají very promptly made an example of him by removing his head from his shoulders.

Wide was the fame of the founder of the power of the Maráthás amongst that race, and great was the spoil. Panalla and Pawan Gurh became his, together with other fortalices, and he levied black-mail down to the banks of the Kistna.

Growing bolder and more adventurous, he ravaged up to the very gates of Bíjápúr, and then turning right about, and dashing like a torrent down the Gháts from the up-lands, he captured Dábul, and bore the plunder of both highlands and lowlands to his mountain. Bent on vengeance for the past, a second army, twice as numerous as the first, was sent against him from Bíjápúr under Salábat Khán, a right good officer, who, with the help of the Sídí chief and the Sawants of Wárí, blockaded him for four months at Panalla until he was desperate. Again the Muhammadans were entrapped by his duplicity, for when they had abandoned their siege-works on the faith of a promised surrender, Sivají rode out with some of his chosen horsemen, and was hotly pursued and in great jeopardy, from which he was preserved by the brave devotion of his former foe Bájí Parvú, who stood like a Maráthá Leonidas in a Hindú Thermopylæ to keep back the headlong assault of the men led by the exasperated Fazl, the son of the late Afzal, who burned to avenge his slaughtered sire. Under cover of this handful of heroes, Sivají rode onwards, and thrice were the enraged assailants driven back. At length numbers gained the day, and the valiant friend of Sivají and half his men lay dead in the pass which they had so well defended; but the survivors made good their retreat, carrying with them the body of their leader, whose last moments had been consoled by the discharge of a gun from Panalla, which announced the safety of his master. Mingling blood and slaughter with the performance of the most superstitious rites, Sivají fought on until he possessed the entire Konkan, from Kallian to Goa, and the Ghâts from the Búná to the Warna. With nearly 60,000 horse and foot, he made Rairí his chief stronghold, and then began systematically to carry on a devastating warfare through the districts of the Mughals. When obliged to abandon Chákan to Shaistah Khán, he surprised that general in Púná, wounded him, and mockingly retired ere the astonished Mughals had discovered the small number of their midnight adversaries.

The native quarters of Súrat he had sacked during six days; but the sturdy English, under their chief factor Sir George Oxenden, showed such a determined front (A.D. 1664), that they not only saved their own property but a portion of that of the citizens; and as the reward of valour, Aurangzíb exempted the English from a portion of the dues exacted from other merchants. Sivají heard of the death of his father near Badnúr, and he now assumed the style and title of Rájá, and had coins struck in his own name. Now plundering the Mughál ships bound to Mocha, now pillaging the suburbs of Ahmadnagar, now inflicting a sanguinary defeat on the troops of Bíjápúr, Sivají seemed to multiply himself in every direction. With three large ships and no less than eighty-five smaller vessels, he made a sudden descent upon Barsílúr and other sea-ports to the south of Goa, and returned gorged with booty. The only resistance was from the English in Karwar, who would not disburse more than £112 to him, with which he was compelled to be satisfied.

But a serious danger threatened the "Mountain Rat," as the Emperor contemptuously styled Sivají, for although Aurangzíb had hitherto dealt leniently with the mischievous Maráthá, the fleecing such pious Musulmáns as the Mecca pilgrims was an offence not to be overlooked or condoned by the fanatical Sultán of Dehlí. On came two of the best officers of his army, Rájá Jái Singh and Dilú Khán, at the head of a formidable force; they crossed the Narbadda, and, after various adventures, brought Sivají to bay, and compelled him to surrender all the forts and territories he had taken from the Mughals, and to co-operate with Jái

Singh in the subjugation of the State of Bíjápúr, where he did such good service as to merit the thanks of Aurangzíb, who invited him to Court. This was treading on dangerous ground, for the Emperor was like Sivají himself, as slippery as an eel; but relying on the assurance of a safeguard from Jáí Singh, the Maráthá determined to visit the capital, whither he proceeded with an escort of some 1,500 chosen troops, in March 1666. When he arrived near Dehlí he was received with marked slight, inasmuch as only two officers of inferior rank were sent out to welcome him, and he was placed in a comparatively low rank when he presented his "Nazr," or offering of fealty, at Court. This angered him, and he expressed himself with so much indignation on the subject that the Emperor forbade him to appear at Court. This, from an Oriental despot of Aurangzíb's calibre, was a sure precursor of something worse, and so it turned out, for shortly after he was honourably confined in his own dwelling, from which he was not permitted to issue unaccompanied by some of the police-guards.

Aurangzíb freely granted passports to Sivají's people who wished to go southwards, because he thought that by doing so he would place the Maráthá chief entirely in his power.

At last Sivají shammed sick, and was allowed to have medical attendance. Pretending after some time to be convalescent, he gave presents to the Brahmans and physicians, and had several large baskets made up which he daily caused to be filled with confectionery and sent to his friends, or for distribution amongst the religious mendicants who hung about the mosques. After lulling suspicion in this way for some time, he, late one evening, put his son Sambáji into one basket and deposited himself in another, and was then borne by his faithful servitors past his unwary guards, who little suspected that under the guise of sweetmeats the "Firebrand of the Western Gháts" was slipping away from their clutches.

Mounting a horse which awaited him on the outskirts of Dehlí, and taking Sambájí behind him *en croupe*, he made rapidly for Mathurá, where his faithful adherent Tanájí Malúsrai and other well-wishers were anxiously waiting to learn the event. All was ready; the lad Sambájí was consigned to some trustworthy Brahmans, who, after shielding him successfully from all the spies of the Emperor during several months, at last conveyed him in safety to the southern country. After an absence of nine months, Sivají himself reached the Dakhan by a circuitous route and after assuming many disguises; and his escape was so well kown in that country, even before he reached it, that the English factors at Karwar, in a letter dated September 29th, 1666, observe that, "If it be true that Sivají hath escaped, Aurangzíb will quickly hear of him to his sorrow," and so he did; but he temporized, and affected to receive the wily Maráthá again into favour, whilst he retained the fortresses of Singarh and Púrandhar, which were garrisoned by the valiant Rájpúts of Jái Singh.

One of the most daring exploits of the great Maráthá adventurer at this period was the escalade, by night, of the stronghold of Singarh, in which the pertinacious bravery of Sivají and his Máwalís overcame even the determined gallantry of the brave Rájpúts who defended it.

Still unceasing in his antipathy to the Mughals, after again seeking Súrat, he defeated a Mughal army near the Násak Pass, and for the first time levied the "elsaut" of the Maráthás, in the province of Khándesh in 1670. When Satára had fallen into his hands, he took on himself the title and assumed the ensigns of royalty. Making peace with the Imperialists and with Bíjápúr, and continuing his own original simplicity and sobriety, the remainder of his life was devoted to innumerable incursions in every direction; but at last the time came for him to die, and he left the world, after a very short illness, at the age of fifty-three, leaving behind him, to this day, in his native Mahárásbtra, the reputation of a demi-god.

LXVIII.

AN EXPLOIT OF SIVAJÍ.

WHEN Sháistah Khán, the nephew of the famous Núr Mahal (of whom Il Musannif will say but few words, because other scribes have already so voluminously dealt with her, that it would be bringing coals to Newcastle to enlarge still further on her manifold excellencies, treacheries, and varied adventures), was appointed Viceroy of the Southern Land, he found that that evil disciple of the Maráthá race, the untamable and predatory Sivají, had not only looted every Muhammadan town and village he could reach, but had wasted the very suburbs of Aurangábád, and returned safe and sound to Púná!

Burning for revenge, the Mughal troops marched on, but Sivají drew cleverly back, ever harassing them and declining a decisive battle. When Chákar was captured, after a desperate siege, Sháistah Khán acted like a gallant gentleman; and, far from massacring the lieutenant of Sivají, dismissed him with all the honour due to undaunted courage.

Then came a lull in the storm, for the Mughals had begun to dislike these sieges of stubborn hill-forts; and when Sháistah Khán once more put his sword for a time into the scabbard, the Maráthás were again abroad, like a flock of destructive locusts.

There was a great house in the city of Púná, which had been built by a Maráthá chief, and in this mansion Sháistah Khán took up his abode, with every precaution to safe-guard himself against an attack of his feline enemies. All without avail, for, as Púná had no walls, Sivají, under cover of a sham marriage-procession, and the ear-breaking music without which a mild Hindú could not be happily wedded, found his way into the very interior of the dwelling of Sháistah Khán. Wild uproar, shrieks of terrified women! Sháistah Khán tries to escape by lowering himself from the window, but loses one of his fingers from a sword-cut; his son, Abu-l-Fath Khán, and most of his guardians are sent into the next world.

After this foray away goes Sivají, and from the summit of an adjoining fort, surrounded by flaming torches, looks down scornfully on the baffled and discomfited Mughals.

LXIX.

THE END OF SAMBAJÍ THE MARÁTHÁ.

Now Aurangzíb was the wiliest of the descendants of Sháh Bábar, whose better qualities, however, he did not possess; from him an opponent, even of his own family, met no mercy. Bigoted and fanatical to an extent almost unsurpassed even in the annals of his own bigoted co-religionists, whilst he was a wholesale murderer of the Hindús, he crushed those Muhammadan southern monarchies which had hitherto stood as a bulwark of Islam during centuries. Then uprose Sivají, and his wild and rapid hordes of Maráthá horsemen, who were destined to plague him until Sivají expired much in the plight in which Catherine the Great of Russia is reported to have died.

When Sivají was no more, his licentious but gallant son Sambájí baffled the Mughál Emperor and was long a thorn in his side, until Aurangzíb entrapped him into a snare which had been baited with one of that sex which furnished a Delilah to the Sampson of the sons of Israel.

Taken unawares, the brave son of Sivají appeared before Aurangzíb, who proffered to him not only his life, but rank, if he would become a Muhammadan. "May your Prophet be accursed!" replied the bold Hindú.

So then Sambájí was costumed with cap and bells, after the fashion of a "clown-like darwesh," and tied on the back of a camel, with his face to the animal's tail. Led through the camp in this disgraceful guise, he called in vain to the Rájpút soldiers of Aurangzíb to preserve him from further misery. Even when his tongue had been hacked off for blasphemy against the Prophet Muhammad, and when the Mughal monarch offered to spare him if he would become a

Musulmán, he *wrote* "Not if you would give me your daughter in marriage!"

This so exasperated Aurangzíb, that he caused the heart of Sambájí to be torn from his breast, his limbs to be cut and carved into pieces, and then thrown to those hungry pariah dogs who invariably follow an Indian camp. But this savagery, far from serving his purpose, only nerved the Maráthá race to more determined and successful efforts against him, as the subsequent history of his descendants only too clearly shows.

LXX.

GURU NÁNAK, THE GENTLE GURU OF THE SIKHS.

Now when Nának was born in Márí, of Kot Kachwá (or the Castle of the Tortoise) in the land of the Five Rivers, most marvellously, and because his mother, who had hitherto been afflicted with barrenness, had eaten the scraps which remained from the repast of one of those unsainted and vagabond mendicants who still abound in Hind, from his earliest years he displayed unusual precocity. Much attached to the race of "fakírs," to whom he superstitiously attributed his coming into the world, he once gave all the money which his father had confided to him for another purpose to some of these sham-religionists; and his father, whose views were less inclined heavenwards, and to abstract ideas concerning religion, chastised him severely. To wean him from his meditations on other matters, his progenitor built a shop, and started him in business in Bist Jálandhar; but the mania of Nának remained unchanged, and all his belongings soon went to the grasping fakírs. When this contrivance had failed, marriage was had recourse to; but that, too, failed to produce the desired effect, and again he hunted the jungle in company with his beloved fakírs, whose set he soon publicly joined. At the age of only eleven he became one of their chief tutors and had many acolytes.

Pure Deism, and the reconciliation of the Musulmáns with the Hindús, by prohibiting to the latter the worship of graven images, and to the former their rabid intolerance of other creeds, together with the slaughter of that sanctified and horned animal the cow, were amongst his chief tenets; but peace and good-will amongst men, an abhorrence of war amongst those who adored the one great God as he did, and the utter abnegation of self, were also doctrines which had a very Christian ring. He traversed India, and some affirm that he visited Mecca, but that sounds like a very Oriental and untrustworthy legend.

"How darest thou, vile infidel, turn thy feet towards the Holy Ka'bah?" "Turn them, if you can," replied misused Guru, "to where the house of God is not!"

Whilst he admitted the divine mission of Muhammad, which was pretty well for one who had been born a "mild Hindú," he attributed his death to his having been a *beef-eater!* With all due respect to the memory of Nának the gentle, Il Musannif fancies he recollects that the "impostor of Mecca" was poisoned by the agency of a leg of mutton!

To this day beef is generally almost impossible to procure throughout the glorious East, although sheep and fowls abound; and Il Musannif seems to remember that he once met an old French Consular friend, and a very delicate gourmand, in the streets of Damascus, who, in recounting the sad hardships of his exiled condition in the land of Syria, moaned out almost with tears in his eyes, "Mais, conçevez-vous, mon cher, il n'y a pas de *bœuf!* il n'y a pas de *bœuf* dans ce *fichû* pays," for so he profanely styled the country watered by Abanon and Pharpar, rivers of Damascus, "where every prospect pleases and only man is vile," to quote the late Bishop Heber anent the island of Ceylon.

Nának was convinced that Muhammad had only been his own (Nának's) successor, and that it was his special mission to restore all mankind to the worship of God alone. Faith and good works alone paved the way to salvation, and caste weighed as nothing in the scales of the new reformer. He included the transmigration of souls in his revelations, and he departed this life peacefully, in the first year of the reign of Sultán

Akbar, and in the year of our Lord 1539, at the age of 71. His tomb and shrine at Kírtipúr, near Kálanúr, on the banks of the Rávi, is a Holy "Dharms'álá," and place of pilgrimage for his more warlike descendants of the present day, who, although they have long eschewed his doctrines of peace and amity, still venerate the memory of the man who was in reality the founder of their creed!

LXXI.

THE "STEEL AND BLUE" GURU GOVIND.

Now when the Guru Arján, in the time of Sultán Sháh Jahán, had drowned himself in the Rávi in order to escape the oppressions of his enemies, in the year of the Christian era 1607, his son Har Govind became Chief Guru in his stead, and warred with the governors of the Emperor. Sorely did he defeat Mukhlis Khán, who, with a strong force of horse, had been sent to seize him, and this was about the first development of that stern military spirit which has since characterised the Sikhs in after days. But prudent as well as brave, Govind, knowing that the weight of the entire Mughál empire would be brought forward to crush him, sought shelter in the forests of Bátindah, in Hissár, where the soil was parched, and where there was scant of water. Whilst lurking in this wild jungle, many became his proselytes, and with them came the noted brigand Buddha, who had daringly pillaged even the royal stables at Lahore.

Vainly was a strong gathering of troops sent against the Guru in his desert-retreat, and the Imperial troops were shamefully driven back.

Nerved by success, Govind once more crossed the Satlaj, and rallied an army round his standards at Kartárpúr, between the town of Jálandhar and the Biyás river. Utter defeat was again the doom of the royal troops, and Har Govind was foremost in the fray. Still, mistrusting his own resources as inadequate to oppose those of the "King of the Earth," he settled in the mountain-fastness of Híratpúr on the right bank of the Satlaj, and died and was interred there in the year of our Lord 1639.

When Tegh Bahádur had been murdered in Dehlí, his son, the grandson of Har Govind, called Govind Ráo, determined to avenge his murder on the authors of his death, and by a stratagem obtained the head of the slaughtered man from where it had been exposed to the contumely and filthy insults of the Muhammadans of the capital.

Then the fierce goddess Deví appeared in all her terrors to the Guru and touched his sword with her hand, *so that in future all his descendants were destined to conquer with the sword.* In deference to the amicable divinity, Govind initiated his career by the sacrifice of one of his followers, and gathered his *Sikhs* (or "Disciples") round him. On them he inculcated equality, the cessation of caste-distinctions, and an utter disregard of the religions, books, and pilgrimages of the Hindús. Respect was due to Guru Nának alone.

Having thus politely put the low-caste Hindú on a level with the Brahman and Kshatriya, who had formerly been his superiors, he gained the majority of the people to his side, and when men of the higher castes showed their repugnance at this innovation, he quailed not, but assembling his 20,000 Súdras together, and, after dictating many rules, gave to them the proud name of "Khalsá," or "the Chosen Ones." Then he tied his uncut hair in a knot, and added "Singh," or "Lion," to his original appellation, together with the "pahul" of the two-edged dagger. Blue was to be the raiment of the new religionists, and ablutions were strictly enjoined, as they had been since the days of Guru Nának.

Unabashed by many vicissitudes or by the murder of his children, the death of his wife, or the desertion of his followers, he escaped from the fort in which he had been beleaguered, and reached Chamkawah with only forty unswerving adherents in his train; all but five of these were slain in a desperate sally after imbruing their swords deeply in the blood of their besiegers;

but the gallant and warrior Guru, and the few who remained to him, escaped amidst innumerable perils to Machhíwárá.

There, to preserve his life, he was compelled by a Muhammadan Saiyyid *to eat beef*, and escaping thence to Ráíkot, many Sikhs came to join him there. With increased numbers, he did desperate battle with the Sudár of Sarhind, and gained a decisive victory over his adversary.

Then, sheltering himself after the fashion of his ancestor and namesake, Har Govind, in an arid jungle, thirst and hunger discomfited the Musulmáns who thirsted for his blood. When Aurangzíb, who was at that time in Southern India, heard of these doings of the Guru, he ordered him to come to the Dakhan and give an account of himself; and on his road thither he was stabbed to death by a young Pathán, whose father he had slain and whom he had exasperated by his taunts. Still the dying man would not allow his murderer to be slain, saying that the lad had only done his duty by avenging his slaughtered father; and, being determined to die before he should be exposed to the not at all tender mercies of Aurangzíb, he purposely burst the stitches of his wound in the belly and died almost immediately.

So ended "the Steel and Blue" Guru in A.D. 1708, in the city of Nádshar, when Bahádur Sháh ruled the land.

LXXII.

THE ANCIENT RACE OF THE THAGS (OR THUGS).

HERODOTUS speaks, in the seventh book of his history, of a race called the Sagartii, who were of Persian descent, and who "noosed" their enemies in battle with cords made of twisted leather, with which they entangled horse and man. This contrivance seems to Il Musannif to differ in no respect from the "lasso" of the Spanish-Americans. With the Muhammadans they came to Dehlí, and planted murderous colonies throughout the length and breadth of the land of Hind. The seven divisions of which this fearsome race consisted, spoke a dialect peculiar to all Thags, and, although at first Musulmáns, soon initiated folk of Hindú origin into their awful practices, and imbibed many of their heathen and idolatrous superstitions. Whilst adhering to the Kurán, they owned to a belief in the "Goddess of Blood," Bhuwání, because they looked on her name as another for Fatimah, the daughter of their Prophet. They thought that though the evil deity of the necklace of human skulls had no influence over a future state, she yet ruled the destinies of the Thags in this life, and that the Almighty would never punish anyone for obedience to her commands.

Calcutta, *alias* Káli-Káta, *i.e.* Káli's acre, had, it appears, the honour of having given birth to this amiable divinity, who was the wife of Shiva or Mahádeo, and there and elsewhere the great Saturnalian festival of the "Durgá Pújá" is still celebrated in her honour.

The "Man-eater," as her worshippers love to style her in ordinary times, is black and hideous of aspect; but in the society of her husband she no longer quaffs draughts of human blood, but becomes "Gaurí," or "the Fair one." In olden time a horrid demon, Rakat Bíj-dáná by name, devoured the human race as soon as they were born; such a giant was he that when he stood in mid-ocean the waves only washed his waist. Cut in two by the sharp "talwár" of Kálí, from every drop of his gore sprang another fiend, until, wearied and perspiring from her fruitless efforts, the goddess created two beings from the sweat which fell from her, to each of whom she gave the "Rúmál," or "handkerchief," with which, at her command, they at length succeeded in exterminating the demons by strangulation. Then she told them to transmit it to their posterity, and therewith to choke all who were not of their own kith and kin; women, however, were to be left intact; it was forbidden to slay a Brahman, a "Káyath" (or "Writer"), a religious mendicant, and people of many other vocations; but in later times these restrictions ceased to be observed.

To this disregard of their ancient institutions, the Thags of the present day mainly attribute their decline and misfortunes.

The watchful Deví ever took an interest in the welfare of her congenial acolytes, whom she aided in their deeds of blood, by sending omens which, if propitious, nerved them to their murderous task from dread of the wrath of the destroying "She-devil." No touch of pity ever made them swerve; old men and young children were both ruthlessly sacrificed, during their expeditions, as blood-offerings to Deví (or "Bhuwání"). When at home their villages were models of order, their lands well-tilled, and family affection ruled supreme; often their very wives were ignorant of the real nature of their occupation, and their sons were never initiated in Thagí until they had attained their fourteenth or fifteenth year, and then they were so gradually and skilfully decoyed into Thagí, that even the mind of the gentlest amongst them eventually became capable of the most terrible atrocities. Faringíyá, one of the most noted amongst them, and whose name will be found in the works of the late Eugene Sue, was one of the most celebrated of these professional assassins, and very calmly and deliberately did he recount his adventures to that great orignator of the Anglo-Thagí system, the late General Sleeman. He was a fine-looking Brahman, and had received his name, because when a party of General Perron's Frenchmen (or "Faringís") stormed and sacked his native village, his mother, whilst flying from the scene of brutality was seized with the pains of labour, brought him into the world, and named him after their French assailants. Once the beauty of a handmaid of Peshwá Bájí Rao so touched the gallant "Strangler" that he allowed her to proceed scot-free to Kánhpúr; but he was not always of such a gentle mood, for when a beautiful young Mughal girl whom he encountered on the road became so desperately enamoured of him that he could not shake her off, his Brahman conscience was so stricken by the defilement which would ensue from the contact of a Musulmán woman, that he caused her and all her attendants to be "thagged" on the spot.

Faringíyá had at one time been in the service of the celebrated Sir David Ochterlony, with whom he was a great favourite, and his own wife was unaware of her lord's nefarious profession. Many Thags have done good service as soldiers of the East India Company, but such was the devilish fascination of the system in which they had been trained, that they would get a couple of days' leave, join some of their old associates, commit as many murders as possible, and then return with feelings of satisfaction to their military duties.

To gather a band of Thags, and to become a jamadár, or lieutenant, or a subadár, or captain, required much generalship and liberality; above all, the aspirant to these high titles must be a master of diplomacy, and of handsome and commanding exterior, and a consummate actor, who could trace his lineage through many generations, whose blood had flowed through scoundrels since the invention of Thagí in the land of Hind! When these gentlemen met, after having performed púja and eaten the consecrated coarse sugar known as gúr, a female carrying a pitcher of water balanced gracefully on her head, their safe return home was a certainty. If a jackass hee-hawed on their left hand, and then on the right, they were sure that Bhuwání was with them. "What a pity," says Il Musannif, "that they were not always in the neighbourhood of the Asinæum!" Diverse other auguries did they deduce from the beasts of the wilds and the fowls of the air.

On the other hand, the falling off of one of their turbans or pagrís (in their own slang "Aghásí," which has a Turkish sound) either stopped or delayed an expedition. Rain out of season was an especial impediment; a kite just before dawn, a lizard, a cripple, an oil-seller, a woman with an empty water-jar, a leper, or an unhealthy man, were sufficiently bad omens, but to meet a donkey face to face was an unmitigated crusher! To write, however, the whole of their superstitions, of which the name is legion, would far exceed the compass of this book.

Sometimes the Muhammadan and Hindú deceivers quarrelled amongst themselves, and when detected and pursued by exasperated zamíndárs, it is not unusual to see the villagers come to their rescue, inasmuch as they are generally looked on as members of a fraternity highly esteemed by Bhuwání. As has long been the custom in Greece, Italy, and Sicily, with the brigands of southern Europe, these criminals were shielded and sympathised with not only by the villagers, but by the police officers, who shared in their ill-gotten gains after the fashion of Hind. These things, however, only were possible in India under the supremacy of its native governors, and during that "golden age" so vaunted by the idiots or knaves of the Manchester school. Il Musannif has done his best in the limited space of this brief work to show how Indian rulers behaved systematically in those "good old times."

The "rú-mál," or face-wiper, was an unfolded turban, or the waist-cloth. It was doubled to the length of about thirty inches, with a knot formed at the double extremity, and about eighteen inches from that was a slip-knot. The distance between these two knots was regulated by preparing the fatal instrument on the knee, which represented a human neck. The knots gave a firm hold, and when the victim was down, the Thag loosed the slip-knot and gave another twist of the rú-mál round his neck; the next proceeding was to put his foot on the patient's neck, and to tighten the band. "Phank," in the lingo of the Stranglers meant a traveller without property, a *vacuus viator*. "Pangú" was a river Thag, who plied his murderous trade in a boat on the Ganges; "Tapal," a wayside path into which unsuspecting wayfarers were craftily inveigled. A wealthy traveller was "a delicacy," and a poor man "a stick."

When danger was not suspected the palm of the hand was drawn over the mouth downwards, but when the back of the hand was drawn along the chin from the throat outwards, it implied approaching peril. Every murderer had his allotted place. "Sweep the place," was "ready"; "bring fire-wood," "take your places preparatory to the murderous game"; "take out the handkerchief with the betel," and "hand the betel round," were the death signals; and when the corpse, which they likened to "a bundle of straw," was to be "looked after," it was to be buried on the spot.

Infinite were their stratagems to avoid suspicion, and both the rú-mál and the kasí, or pick-axe, were sanctified instruments. Full belief, too, had these scoundrels in their divine mission, and if any one of their number took a false oath on the holy kasí, the care of which was always entrusted to one of the most respected of the Thags, he was sure to die a terrible death, for his head gradually turned round until his eyes looked at his heels! The kasí was, in fact, the standard of Thagí, just as in other times the blacksmith's apron had been the standard of Irán, and was worshipped every seventh day. After every murder, a sacrifice was offered to the blood-drinker, Bhuwání, and great were their preparations and superstitious observances ere they set forth from their villages on their campaign of cold-blooded murder. Their chiefs, under various well-carried-out disguises, acquired the confidence of the unwary as they trudged along the hot and dusty roads to Banáras, or elsewhere, and few of them bore arms. Once they scented their prey they followed their victims like blood-hounds, as they were, and hardly ever failed in their object. Bhuwání, the amiable, was kind enough to succour her votaries by causing the corpses of the strangled to disappear; and even one farthing, or two pice, was a sufficient temptation to break down the temple of life. Still there was "honesty among thieves," and Thags frequently rendered back spoils to which other comrades were entitled by the rules of the Stranglers.

Il Musannif has no space left to deal at length with their feasts in honour of Deví, whilst engaged in an expedition, and must now say something of the Water Thags, who generally prowled up and down the Ganges as far as Kánhpúr, and affected to be peaceable boat-owners, or merchants. Their sothás, or decoys, inveigled travellers on board their boats, and the Bangú crew and pretended voyagers seated themselves in a row on the deck, facing their intended victims. Then the signal of execution was given by the helmsman; and when strangulation had taken place, assurance was made doubly sure by the fracture of the spine. Out then went the defunct into the rapid current of the broad river; property which might have been identified was destroyed, and no blood was shed. The murdered corpses were indistinguishable from the myriads of half-roasted Hindú bodies which infest the majority of Indian rivers, and soon kites, crows, vultures, crocodiles, and jackals were furnished with fresh provender. Yet the rascally Hindústání police, whose eyes were blinded by the bribes of the Bangús, persistently kept facts, which had long been known to them, until the year of grace 1836, when effective measures began to be taken to check this system of Thagí, which was the most difficult of detection of all the schemes of the ancient race of the deceivers.

To prove what wholesale murder was habitually perpetrated, Il Musannif may mention that, on one occasion, twenty Thags who had been admitted as Guyindahs, or informers, acknowledged that they were respectively present at 508, 931, 350, 377, 604, 119, 42 (a very small man of business!), 103, 264, 203, 195 294, 117, 322 340, 28 (a still more despicable murderer) 65, 81, 153 and 24 other murders. The average of this butcher's bill amounted to 256 murders to each of the score of Thags. When in 1830 Farangíyá was brought before Captain Sleeman, on condition that he should give such information as would lead to the capture of others of his brethren of the cord, he, on the second stage out of Ságar, whence he accompanied the British officer on his official tour of inspection, pointed out, in the very mango-grove in which Sleeman's tents were pitched, the graves of three batches of poor wretches in whose slaughter he had ably assisted. Says the English officer: "A pandit and his six attendants, murdered in 1818 (twelve years before), lay among the ropes of my sleeping-tent; a havildar and four sipáhís, slain in 1824, lay under the hoofs of my horses; and four Brahman-carriers of Ganges water, and a woman, lay beneath my sleeping tent; the sward had grown over the whole! All night long Mrs. Sleeman had tossed about in her sleep, tormented by horrible dreams, probably engendered by the foul air produced by so many graves."

The prudence and tact of this abominable brood were worthy of a Talleyrand. Europeans were strictly avoided by them, not only on account of the peril likely to result from armed resistance, but for fear of the searching inquisition which would assuredly follow the disappearance of a white man. All tell-tale property was speedily destroyed, and murders were never perpetrated in the vicinity of their own part of the country. The vast population of Hindústán was always on the move. Parties of travellers or solitary foot or horsemen streamed along the roads and bye-paths, reposing during the heat of the day, or during the dark hours of the night, beneath the clumps or topes of trees which abound everywhere in Hind, and rarely failed to become the victims of those whose apparent good-fellowship stifled suspicion. Only eighty years have elapsed since the Phánsígars of the south became known to the English, but at that time their profession was not suspected of being an hereditary one, and it was only in 1829–30 that thorough measures for the extermination of these infamous assassins were taken by Lord William Bentinck, then Governor-General; and now it has almost entirely disappeared.

In conclusion, Il Musannif begs to quote the words of an able modern writer on the topic:—

"Let British supremacy in India cease when it will, the suppression of Thagí will ever remain a glorious monument to the zeal, energy, and judgment of the civil and military servants of the East India Company, and the impartial student of Indian history can readily adduce many such examples as the preceding—for instance, the suppression of Satí, human sacrifices, and infanticide, the repression of torture, gang-robberies, and voluntary mutilation—in order to prove that these merchants were truly princes and amongst the honourable of the earth."

LXXIII.

THE DAKÁÍTS OF HINDÚSTÁN.

When that land of Hind which is now governed by the Franks or Faringís was in the unclean hands of its former masters, murder and robbery were professions which were handed down from father to son throughout scores of generations, and when the Thags had been suppressed, the hereditary robbers or Dakáíts proved more difficult of extinction. Oudh (or "Awadh"), and, in fact, any state over which the flag of the Honourable Company did not fly, were the resorts of brigands, who, living as they did in the depths of tangled and almost inaccessible jungles, swooped unexpectedly, as does the hawk from his eyrie, on the prey, and then disappeared with equal promptitude before any pursuit could be organised. As did the Thags, so did the Dakáíts, whose disguises were infinite and suited to the localities through which they prowled, taking advantage of the superstitious observances of India; they were, as their purpose demanded, sham mourners or pilgrims, and their daring and insolent attacks upon Government treasure-parties were only too often attended with success. Long impunity, and that sordid venality of the Indo-British police, which has so long been a blemish on the rule of those Europeans (who, though true and earnest themselves in the suppression of crime, can scarcely ever rely on their knavish subordinates), allowed the Dakáíts, —who were invariably well-armed men and generally numerous,—to continue their ravages; but when Sleeman, "the Exterminator of Thagí," took the matter in hand, a great change was soon seen, and the

Upper Provinces of the Bengal Presidency were rapidly freed from their former pests. In the Lower Provinces, in the delta of the Ganges, Dakáití can scarcely be said to be extinguished yet, but its days are numbered, and it diminishes year by year.

LXXIV.

A NEST OF PROFESSIONAL THIEVES AND THEIR WORTHY RÁJÁ.

When Major F. Harris, Superintendent of Chandairí, wrote to the Rájá of Bánpúr concerning the professional Sunoreah thieves, who were not only tolerated but protected by him, and who made incursions into the Company's territories, to the great detriment of industrious and law-abiding people. This extract from the reply of the Hindú chief,—which thoroughly exemplifies morality and good government from a native point of view,—will show how little the present rulers of Hind can rely on the faith or honesty of the upper classes of India.

"I have to state that from former times these people following their professions, have resided in my territory and in the states of other native princes, and that they have always followed this calling, but no former kings or princes have ever forbidden this practice; therefore, these people for generations have resided in my territory and in the states of other princes, proceeding to distant districts to follow their occupation, robbing by day for a livelihood for themselves and families, both cash and any other property they could lay their hands on. *In consequence of these people stealing by day only, and that they do not take life, or distress any person by personal ill-usage, and that they do not break into houses, but simply by their smartness manage to abstract property, I looked on such petty thefts as trifles, and have not interfered with them.*"

This fine old Hindú gentleman, moreover, calmly admits that he shared in the ill-gotten spoils of the Sunoreahs, and in this he was imitated by a certain Rájá not very long ago;—if Il Musannif mistakes not, it was the father of that Rájá who became the *confrère* of these "area-sneaks," and spent some of his plunder in this country.